ALL MY DAYS

Kathleen Dayus was born in Hockley, Birmingham, in 1903. Her childhood, vividly recalled in the award-winning first volume of her autobiography, *Her People* (Virago 1982), was spent in the city slums, in a district of small engineering works and metal-working foundries known as 'The Jewellery Quarter'. Her early life was one of appalling poverty, inadequate food and cramped living conditions in one of the densely populated courts built to house Birmingham's working poor. She left school at the age of fourteen. Kathleen's life once she embarked upon the world of work was taken up in the second volume of her autobiography, *Where There's Life* (Virago 1985): odd jobs, presswork in factories, munitions work during the war, later enamelling. In 1921 she married; ten years later, with four small children, she was left a widow, and was forced onto the money-lender, then parish relief before eventually she had to relinquish her children to the care of Dr Barnado's homes. For eight years she struggled to make an independent living so that her children might return. Her life after those gruelling years establishing her own thriving business are largely the subject of this, the third volume of her remarkable autobiography.

Now in her mid-eighties, Kathleen Dayus still lives in Birmingham, and has twelve grandchildren and eight great-grandchildren.

KATHLEEN DAYUS

ALL MY DAYS

Published by VIRAGO PRESS Limited 1988
20–23 Mandela Street, London NW1 0HQ

Reprinted 1989

British Library Cataloguing in Publication Data

Dayus, Kathleen, *1903—*
All my days.
I. Title
942.4'96

ISBN 0-86068-076-2

Typeset by Goodfellow & Egan Ltd, Cambridge
Printed and bound in Great Britain
by Cox and Wyman Ltd, Reading, Berkshire

Contents

Preface

In this book I have once again written about my own experiences, and told the stories of the loves and lives I held, and hold, dear. And my wishes are that this book, like my two previous books, will help to bring back memories to older people. And convey to the younger ones a true picture of how the people of my generation lived.

I wish to thank all my relatives and many kind friends, past and present, who should never be forgotten.

KATHLEEN DAYUS
Birmingham, 1988

1

Tales of Childhood

I am now in my eighty-fourth year, and I often find myself thinking of my childhood. I was born in Birmingham in 1903, and I grew up with people who, like my own family, lived in dire poverty, in disease-ridden slums. They had to bear hardships always, and tragedies often. But these people had a determination to survive, whatever the cost. It was this, coupled with a sense of humour, which enabled them to get through a life of existence.

*

The day I was five years old my mother registered me at the local school. I remember my teacher, who was a small, dumpy person, very stern and forbidding, with a weather-worn, wrinkled skin which made her look older than her years. She was never seen without a bamboo cane carried at the ready.

We were taught our ABC sitting on bare wooden floors which always smelt strongly of disinfectant. Many of us kids didn't even have bloomers or knickers, and if teacher happened to notice us with our legs apart, she would rap our knees with the cane.

'Disgusting,' she'd yell out for all the other kids to hear. 'Showing all you've got! It's disgraceful the way some of you girls are sent to school! Tell your mothers, aunts, or sisters, or whoever's in charge of you, to find you some kind of bloomers! Otherwise I shall send you back home next time you come.'

The kids who were lucky enough to own a pair of bloomers would titter and call after us:

Maggie Brown's got no drawers
Will yer kindly lend her yowers

When I got home one Friday afternoon, I told my mum that the teacher had said she would send me home if I came again without bloomers.

'Yer'll afta buy 'er a pair Polly,' I heard my dad say to Mum.

'Buy 'er a pair?' she yelled. 'Where do yer think the money comes from? It don't grow on trees, yer know.'

'Well, try an' mek 'er a pair out o' my old striped union shirt. It's beyond patchin', any'ow,' Dad replied.

'I was goin' ter cut that up fer towels,' she answered.

No more was said. Dad went out to fetch in the tin bath from off the outside wall, for Friday night was my bath night. As I sat splashing myself all over in the warm carbolic soapy water, I noticed Mum had already begun to cut up the shirt, and was trying to codge two legs together, as she sat by the fire facing me.

I remember wearing those monstrosities until they had gone too far to be patched any more. Sometime later, one of our neighbours was lucky enough to buy an old second-hand sewing machine. Soon after that all the neighbours pooled their pennies and bought some brown calico and made all us unfortunates new bloomers. But I was only allowed to wear these when I went to church, or Sunday School. For everyday school I had to wear my codged-together ones.

When we were a bit older we moved up off the floor to long dark oak forms, which seated four. Raised above each form was a lean-to ledge, with a slot for our wooden pens, and four holes which held our crock ink wells. Everything always smelt of disinfectant or paraffin.

Our teachers were very strict, and strong on discipline: but there was nothing they could do about how we lived or dressed, as long as we had clean heads, and bodies free from vermin.

One day at school I began to itch all over. My teacher noticed me scratching, and with a scowl on her face she called me out in front of the class. As I stood beside her, she said loudly, for all to hear, 'Have you got fleas? If you have, you had better sit in the back row.'

'No, miss. I just itch,' I answered nervously.

'Turn around, and face the class!' she said sternly.

Keeping me at arm's length, she lifted my hair with a pencil; when she'd had a good look, she gave me a hard poke with her thumb in the middle of my back.

'Now get back to your seat. And don't let me see you scratching again, or I'll send you to the clinic.'

I knew all the other girls' eyes were on me, as I held my head down and walked slowly back to my seat. I felt ready to cry. I was glad when I looked up at the clock that hung on the wall over the blackboard, and saw that it read a minute to twelve. That next minute seemed like an hour, until teacher took up the iron bell from her desk to let us know it was time to march in single file down the narrow dark corridor, and out into the street.

I was still tearful as I entered our house, hoping Mum was not at home. But she was standing black-leading the grate. As she had her back towards me I took the opportunity to give my back a good hard rub against the edge of the wooden sofa. Suddenly she turned round and saw me.

'What's up with yer now?' she yelled.

'I itch all over, Mum, an' now me back feels sore,' I whimpered.

When she had looked at my back, she said she was taking me to see the doctor.

'Can't 'e come 'ere, Mum, yer know I'm scared of doctors.' (Our neighbours often called a doctor a 'quack' or a 'butcher', or an 'old sawbones'.)

'No 'e can't,' she snapped. 'I ain't got coppers ter waste on visits.'

She grabbed my hand and hurried me along to see Dr Mackay, who lived in a bow-windowed shabby old house, just around the corner, with his wife and three children. He did all his consulting in his front room, and his back room was the dispensary, where his wife gave out bottles of medicine or whatever was needed. You didn't have a prescription to take to a chemist in those days.

His visits were as low as sixpence, but even that was a lot for poor people to pay; you could get a couple of meals for sixpence in those days.

Mum and I sat on the long, hard form in the narrow corridor, which smelt strongly of disinfectant. There were several other women waiting their turn, with small children and babies in arms. When it was our turn, Mum stopped whispering to the woman next to her, and almost dragged me in. The doctor was a large, thick-set man, with unruly red hair and moustache. I began to tremble with fear, wondering what he was going to do or where he would send me. He frowned over the top of his spectacles, first at Mum, then at me, then, turning his gaze on Mum again, he snapped 'Well?'

'I've brought me daughter fer yer ter see, doctor. Yer see, she keeps scratchin' 'erself.'

'Take her behind the screen and take her clothes off,' he snapped impatiently.

Quickly Mum undressed me, taking off all but my threadbare shift. As I stood there shivering with fear and cold, she went to tell him that I was ready. As soon as he saw me he told Mum to take off my shift, and there I stood, naked. I looked away and closed my eyes. When it was my bath night, I always felt dirty when I looked down at my nakedness. Now here I stood, as naked as I was born, with this man staring down and prodding me. I couldn't for the life of me open my eyes until he'd stopped. Then I heard him say to my Mum, 'Get her dressed at once, and wait in the corridor until I bring you out some powder.'

'What's 'er got, then?' I heard Mum ask, as I hurriedly fumbled to get dressed.

'Chicken pox.' he snapped.

While we waited in the corridor again, one of the women asked Mum what was wrong with me. I expected her to say 'Mind yer own bloody business,' but she didn't for once. When she cried out 'Chickenpox' I saw everyone move away from us quickly.

When the doctor gave Mum the powder he told her to dab it on the chickenpox sores twice a day. For four weeks I stayed away from school, with Mum roughly dabbing my neck, back and chest. I was also kept isolated from the rest of the family. This meant I couldn't sleep in the same bed as my brother and sister, so I had a bed made up for me on the wooden sofa downstairs. During those four weeks my Mum had a regular jaunt to the school clinic for bottles of disinfectant to wash our clothes with, and use around the rooms.

When I got well again I started back to school. But three weeks later I was sent home with a sore throat. I was too scared to tell my Mum in case she took me to see the doctor again, but at school the next day I vomited all down my frock, and my teacher gave me the cane and sent me home.

As soon as Mum saw the state I was in, she cried out, 'What yer bin eatin' now?'

'Nothin', Mum, but me throat is sore. *Please,*' I pleaded, *'please don't tek me ter that doctor again.'*

'Open yer mouth an' let's look,' she shouted.

She blew some dry sulphur powder down my throat, then she dragged in the tin bath from off the wall outside. I had a bath, then I was sent straight to bed.

'An' yer can stay theea, until I can find time ter see ter yer!' she yelled impatiently.

Although I cried as I climbed the attic stairs, I was pleased she didn't take me to see the doctor again. But I was still feeling sick and restless. I couldn't even swallow my spittle without it hurting me. Later that afternoon, I plucked up my courage and, regardless of what my mum would say or do to me, I got out of bed and went downstairs.

'Mum,' I cried, as I sat on the stairs, 'I think I'm goin' ter die, I can't swaller, an' my throat feels on fire.'

She soaked one of my dad's old woollen socks in camphorated oil and pinned it around my throat, then sent me back upstairs again.

During the night I tossed and turned. My throat was so hot and dry, I felt I must have a drink. But I was scared to wake my mum and ask her: waking her at any time was the worst thing any of us could do. So, not to disturb my brother and sister who slept in the same bed, I crept slowly and silently out of bed and reached for the piece of candle that was kept on the orange-box beside the bed. Barefoot and in my threadbare shift, I crept quietly down the stairs. When I reached the first floor landing I didn't feel quite so nervous, for I could hear Mum and Dad sending the pigs home to market. When at last I crept into the living room I got a piece of paper and from the hot embers I managed to light the piece of candle. I looked up at the mantleshelf at the alarm clock which only had one hand. I saw that it was pointing between twelve and one, so it was now about half past twelve. We didn't have water laid on in the house, so I tried the kettle on the hob, but it was bone dry. There was only one thing left for me to do. I slipped Mum's black shawl over my head and shoulders and, picking up a mug from the table, I went out to get some water from the tap in the yard. I didn't need the lighted candle now. It was a lovely moonlit night, and the gas lamp in the yard lit up all the houses and the yard. I drank three mugs straight down of that delicious cold water. I had just filled the mug again to take indoors, and was about to cross the yard, when I heard the sound of cartwheels coming down our narrow cobbled street. Scared, I hid behind the wall that divided the back-to-back houses, but as I peeped over it, I could see quite clearly two ragged individuals, a man and a woman, pushing a flat hand-cart with their few chattels: two wooden chairs, a table, two straw mattresses, an iron bedstead, and other odd utensils. Following close behind were a small boy and girl, who, I was to find out later were my age and were twins.

"urry yerselves, yow two kids,' I heard the man say. 'We ain't got all night.'

I realised that this family, like a good many more families in those days, were doing a moonlight flit. As I peeped from my hiding place, I saw the man and woman push the hand-cart into the next yard and enter the empty house at the back of ours. These people were to be our new neighbours.

Shivering with the cold night air, I hurried indoors. After throwing off Mum's old black shawl, I drank the other mug of water and quietly crept back upstairs again. By now my throat had cooled down a little, and it didn't seem to be quite so painful.

I looked down at my brother and sister, and, glad to see they were still asleep, I snuggled down on the warm mattress beside them. Soon I fell asleep too. The next thing I knew, Mum was yelling up the attic stairs.

'Yow betta 'urry yerselves, yow three, fer school, afower I come up theea an' tip yer out.'

My sister and brother leapt out of bed first. I would never dress or undress in front of them, so I waited. Then as soon as they went down the stairs I jumped out of bed and began to dress quickly. When I was only half-dressed I happened to glance into the piece of looking glass that hung over the small fireplace. I got the shock of my life. Staring at me I saw another face with narrow slits for eyes. Quickly I looked around the room expecting to see someone there, but there was no one. When I looked into the mirror again and put my hands up to feel if it was *my* face I could see, I got scared. My face and neck were twice their normal size, and my puffed eyes were just slits. Screaming, and half-naked, I ran down the stairs.

'Mum! Mum!' I screamed, aghast. 'Look at me face!'

'Oh, my God!' she yelled out, 'Yow've got mumps!'

So, with another sock and a smothering of more of that vile-smelling camphorated oil, I was hurried back to bed again.

I couldn't settle to lie down in bed. The smell from the sock was so awful I could almost taste it. I needed air, so I got out of bed and pushed up the attic window, and as I looked down into the yard below, I saw my Mum with several of the neighbours. Through snatches of overheard conversation I discovered they were discussing our new neighbour.

I hadn't been standing there for long when Mum happened to glance up and see me at the window. Before I could fly back into bed she was in the room.

'Get yerself down in that bed at once!' she shrieked. 'An' if I catch yer out again yer'll feel the back of me 'and.'

Scared, I slid down underneath the bedclothes and stayed there until I heard her slam the window down and return downstairs.

I had to stay in bed for two whole weeks. But I was glad about one thing: I had the bed to myself. Liza and Frankie had to sleep in Mum's room, on a makeshift bed on a straw mattress.

Kind neighbours sent whatever titbits they could spare, and, with Mum's home-made concoctions, my face soon came back to its normal size. Although I was very pale and thin, I wanted to go back to school, for I was missing my playmates. But when I asked my mum, she snapped at me 'No! Yer can't go yet, yer can 'ave another few days 'elpin' me with the washin'.'

I followed her down the yard, where she handed me the bucket.

'Yer can start fillin' this, an' bring it in the brew'ouse.'

It was a heavy galvanised bucket, one my dad had brought home from somewhere. I'd got it half filled, and was about to carry it to the brewhouse when I dropped it quick, and ran behind the brewhouse door for cover.

'What's the matter with yer now? An' where's the bucket o' water?'

'Ssh, Mum,' I whispered. 'The school board man's knockin' our door.'

'Well, yer betta stop theea till 'e's gone.'

We both watched as he knocked several times on our door. Getting no answer, he walked away. He came back the following afternoon just as Dad was soaking his feet in a bowl of hot water. As soon as I saw him, I hid on the stairs. When he knocked, Dad called out, 'Come in.'

'I've come about your daughter,' he said at once. 'She's not attended school for three weeks, so I've come to warn you, if you don't send that child to school you'll be having a summons.'

'The missus couldn't send 'er, she's 'ad mumps,' was Dad's reply.

'Well, you have to send in a doctor's note,' he answered.

Dad said he hadn't got coppers to spare for a doctor's note, but he would see that I went next day. Mum and Dad quarrelled. In the end she promised him I would go next day. But she still kept me to help in the house.

A week later Dad received the summons. He was fined half a crown and given seven days to pay it. But the good, kind neighbours rallied round, and with their few pennies they were able to pay his fine.

After more quarrels I was happy to be back at school. But I found some of the girls kept their distance from me, afraid they would catch what I had lost. I snubbed them in return. Then, as I stood alone in the playground, a little red-haired girl came up to me.

'Yow 'ad mumps?' she asked at once.

'Yes,' I snapped, 'an' what's it ter do with yow? An' who are yow? I've never seen yer before.'

'Me name's Winnie Nashe, I live in the next yard.'

'Ooh, I remember, yer the new people come ter live in number nine.'

'Yes. Want a piece o' toffee?' she asked as she handed me a piece of treacle toffee.

'Thank you, but yer betta not let teacher see yer suckin' it or yer'll get the cane.'

'I'd like ter see 'er or anybody else lay a finger on *me*, an' they'll get what for.'

She was quite a little spitfire, but I liked her, and from then on we became good friends. We went almost everywhere together, and shared whatever we had. She was just three months older than me, and the same height. But, apart from that, we were as different in looks, as chalk is from cheese. I had long dark hair, and I was pale and thin. She was plump, with a round, rosy face covered with freckles. And she was very pretty.

I took her home one day to meet my mum. Mum usually didn't like the girls who called for me, but I was pleased to see she took to Winnie at once.

As we were walking up the hill, we met Winnie's twin brother, Willie. He was so much like Winnie, you couldn't tell them apart, only that he wore much too large ragged trousers, well below his knees.

When we left school the following day Winnie said she had to hurry home to help her mum. I didn't want her to. I said I wanted someone to talk to.

'Would yer like ter come 'ome an' meet my mum, then?' she asked.

'Will she mind?' I asked.

'Course she won't, I told 'er yesterday I'd bring yer sometime, so come on, don't be shy,' she said, as she took my hand.

As we passed our yard I told her I would have to call and tell my mum where I was going. There was only Frankie at home.

'Frankie,' I said, 'will yer tell me mum if she wants me I'll be round the back in Winnie's 'ouse.'

'All right, but mind what yer up to,' he replied.

'Who's that 'ansome lad yer spoke to?' Winnie asked.

'Me brother,' I answered.

'I could fall fer 'im,' she giggled. 'Come on if yer comin'.'

When we got to Winnie's I was surprised to see such an untidy house. Everything seemed to be cluttered about everywhere. There were old coats thrown over chairs, and strips of cloth strewn across the table. Squatting on the floor sat Winnie's mum and dad. They too had red hair. And when they both stood up they looked like Tweedle Dum and Tweedle Dee.

'Come an' sit down if you can find room, an' would you like a cuppa tea?' Winnie's mum asked.

'Yes, please,' I answered.

'Put the kettle on the fire then, Winnie, while I get the things in off the line.'

What I expected to see her bring in was a basket full of washing, but instead she had an armful of old grey, black and brown coats that she gave to her husband to cut into strips.

On the way home, I asked Winnie what her dad did for a living.

'Oh, 'e's in the rag trade,' she said.

'What yer mean, the rag trade?'

'Well, 'e's really a rag and bone man, but when anybody asks, we all say that, because it sounds better.'

'But what's yer mum and dad cut the coats into strips for?'

'Well, Mum makes peg rugs, and sells them fer a shillin'. Sometimes when she gets an order, I take one, or maybe two, and charge another tuppence, which I keep fer meself,' she added.

So that was why she always had plenty of sweets to share with me.

One day during the summer, I went with her to take two rugs to a woman who lived a few streets away. When Winnie knocked on the door she came out and said she was sorry, but she only wanted one.

'But me mum said yer wanted two.'

'I'm sorry, dear,' I heard her say, 'but my sister's changed her mind.'

'Yer can 'ave 'em both fer two an' tuppence,' Winnie said.

'I only want the one, or not at all,' she replied firmly.

'Very well,' Winnie replied, an' thank yer.'

She gave her the peg rug, and took the one and tuppence.

As she walked down the path Winnie dropped the two pennies down her stocking, and said she would try to sell the other one next door. She lifted the brass knocker. But the woman who came to the door shouted at us, 'Be off with yer or I'll set the bloody dog on yer.'

'Yer can 'ave it fer a shillin', Winnie said.

'I don't want it!' she yelled again.

When she tried to shut the door Winnie pleaded, and pushed the door wider. But as soon as we saw the bull terrier growling at us in the hall, we ran for our lives. When we glanced back we saw the dog was gaining on us. Now, Winnie wasn't able to run as fast as me, for she was carrying the rug. But as soon as the dog got near enough, she turned around and flung the rug at him and fled. When we got some distance away, we looked back to see the rug going around in circles with the dog beneath, trying to free himself. Then we hurried to explain to her mum what had happened.

'Never mind, as long as he didn't bite you,' was all she said.

The next day, Winnie told me her dad had found the rug lying in the gutter, so he brought it home in the cart.

A while later Winnie's mum had to go into the infirmary for an operation, and my mum said Winnie could stay with us until she came home again. Mum made up a makeshift bed so that Winnie and I could sleep together, and we had great fun telling stories and reading from the comic strips. We were both so happy – for a few days. Then the school nurse came to examine all our heads

and bodies, and when she saw Winnie and I had scabies, we were
sent home at once. Mum was furious. All the neighbours knew
now from the other kids, so they kept their distance. When the
health man came that afternoon, he said we and Mum too, would
have to go to the clinic to be cleansed.

I shall never forget the humiliation we suffered that day. When
we arrived, Mum was sent into one room and Winnie and me
were taken into another. We were stripped naked, and all our
clothes, and even our boots, were taken away to be fumigated.
We were embarrassed, trying not to look at each other's naked
bodies.

When the nurse came in, she took us into an almost bare
whitewashed room which contained a large enamel bath full of
steaming hot water. As we stood there, trying to hide our private
parts with our hands, she poured disinfectant from a large blue
bottle into the bath. We were fascinated by the way the
disinfectant turned the water almost white, like milk. Then the
nurse made us jump, calling out impatiently, 'Come on! Get in,
yow two!'

But we jumped out quicker than we went in: the bath water
was so strong, it almost burnt our flesh. However, there was no
escape. With her two strong hands she pushed us roughly into the
water, and with the hard brush she scrubbed us from head to foot.
When she thought we'd had enough she lifted us out, and took us
dripping wet into another room. This too was bare but for an iron
pipe stove that was belching smoke. We gazed at one another.
We had begun to weep, wondering what she was going to do to us
next, when she came back into the room with a bucket of what
looked like whitewash, a large brush, and a coarse calico towel.

'Dry yerselves with this, then follow me,' she called out as she
threw the towel towards us.

As we followed behind her, we tried to cover our naked bodies
by wrapping the towel around ourselves. But it was soon snatched
away.

'Yer don't afta be shy in front of me! I 'ave lots more than this
ter deal with. Now 'urry up, I ain't got all day!' she cried out
impatiently.

This room too was bare as we entered. We were told to stand in the middle of the room, and, using the brush, she slapped the white paste all over each of us in turn. She seemed to be enjoying this job, smiling at each stroke. We were left again until the paste had dried. Then we were handed our clothes (which had been fumigated), and we got dressed. We met Mum in the hall. She was shouting and swearing at the nurse, and the attendants, ' about the state of our clothes that we had to walk home in.

The three of us felt ashamed to walk down our street, so Mum took us the long way round to avoid the nosy neighbours. When we got home, Mum told us to take off our frocks and she would iron out the creases. Later that same day, she went back to the clinic to fetch her supply of disinfectant for the home. This disinfectant was called Condy's Fluid. It was very powerful stuff, but Mum hid it away and only used it sparingly. Half a spoon in the washing, the same in the water used for cleaning the bedroom and attic, and a drop in the slop bucket we kept beside the bed, in case we were cut short in the night.

2

Growing Up

As soon as Mrs Nashe came home from the infirmary, Mum sent Winnie packing. Mum said it was their fault we had got scabies, through the old coats they collected, and I was forbidden to have anything more to do with Winnie, or go near their house. After that Winnie never came to our house for me, and I never went to hers. All the same, unbeknownst to Mum, I often met her outside school hours. But a few weeks later I was upset to find that Winnie and her family had left the district.

It was some months before I saw her again. Then one afternoon, as I was busy scrubbing the stairs, there came a couple of taps on the door. At first I was afraid to answer it. I asked myself, was it someone for my dad for the debts he owed? For Mum had warned me if anyone called while she was out I was not to answer, or if I had to I must just say my dad had gone away, and I didn't know where. But whoever it was this time wouldn't leave, they just kept on knocking. Slowly I opened the door a little, and I was about to ask who it was when I was surprised to see my old friend Winnie. At first I hardly recognised her. She'd quite grown up. Where I was still straight up and down and flat-chested, she had developed a bust which seemed to burst through her too-tight faded brown velvet frock. And her hair, which had been fiery red, had changed to a rich auburn. I noticed that she still had plenty of freckles, though.

She cried out, 'Don't stand there gawpin' at me, don't yer know me?'

'Yes, of course I do, Winnie, but my, how you've changed.'

'Ain't yer goin' ter call me in then?' she asked.

'Yes, Winnie, but I never expected ter see yer – not terday, anyroad. Well, come on in, an' pull up a chair by the fire, while I put me bucket away, an' mek a pot o' tea.'

Winnie told me that she was back living in the next street, and she would be coming back to our school on Monday. I told her that I was now in Standard Six, with a new teacher, Mrs Frost. I liked Mrs Frost. She was strict, but kind if you tried to do things right. The only trouble was, she tried to make us sound our aitches, and generally 'talk posh', as we called it. This was easy enough when you were repeating words in class, but as soon as you got home, with your mum and dad and all the neighbours talking Brummy slang, it became impossible. It was like speaking another language.

A while after Winnie returned, I was soaping my chest one bath night when I became scared. I felt two hard lumps around my nipples, and they were painful to touch. I couldn't tell my mum in case she took me to see the doctor again. But I had to tell someone. Winnie was my only hope. Next morning when she called for me to go to the park, I began to weep. When she asked why I was crying, I said, 'I can't go out with yer terday, Winnie, I've got these awful pains around me nipples.'

''ow long 'ave yer 'ad 'em?' she asked.

'Well, I only felt 'em last night when I 'ad me bath.'

'Yer betta let me 'ave a look,' she said.

I was too shy to show her, so I asked her if she knew what was wrong with me.

'I don't know, do I, unless I look at 'em!' she snapped.

'All right, I'll shut me eyes while yer look.'

When I pulled up my frock and she felt my breasts, I began to feel dirty, and cringed. But she put me at ease, when I heard her laugh out loud and say, 'Yer can put yer frock down an' open yer eyes. Yer silly little fool – yer know what's wrong with yer? *Nothin'*. It's the start of yer titties growin', but they're only lemon drops yet. You wait till they grow like mine.'

'Ooh, I don't want 'em to grow out like yowers,' I replied. 'I wouldn't know what clothes ter wear.'

'You will when the time comes. My mum tells me if I grow 'em any bigger, I'll afta wear a camisole an' a pair of stays.'

I was relieved to know it was only the beginning of my little 'lemon drops' or my 'titties' as she called them.

Some of the girls at school went to swimming classes, and one afternoon Winnie asked me if I'd ever been swimming.

'Never,' I said. 'Why do yer ask?'

'Well, we go to the public swimming baths on Wednesday afternoons.'

'I don't think my mum would let me go.'

'She wouldn't know if yer dain't tell 'er. Anyway, it's better than a tin bath, yer can't swim in a tin bath, an' teacher says it develops yer body muscles, an' Katie, yours sure needs developin', yer such a skinny little thing fer yer age.'

'But I can't swim, an' I ain't got a costume,' I replied.

'Yer can borrow my old one, it's too small for me now. It's only a penny. I'll treat yer. Say now yer'll come.'

'But I've told yer, I can't swim.'

'Yer can learn. There's always an instructor there with a long pole.'

Well, I thought, here goes. If Winnie could swim, it was about time I learned. So the following Wednesday afternoon I went with Winnie and the other girls to Northward Street baths.

Winnie paid my penny to the attendant, but when she handed me a towel she looked down her nose at me. 'Yer a new 'un, ain't yer? Well, see as yer scrub yer feet befower yer go in the baths.'

After Winnie and I scrubbed our feet in the large basin, we had to undress in a shared cubicle. It wasn't really large enough for one person, let alone two of us. There was hardly room to turn round. It had half a door that swung outwards and inwards, and it wasn't very private, anyone passing could see our faces, and our feet and legs. But we managed to undress.

When Winnie handed me the costume I was to wear, I was disappointed. It had dark brown and yellow wide stripes. Any other time I wouldn't have been seen dead in it. But Winnie had meant to be kind. I couldn't hurt her feelings by refusing to wear it, so I put it on, but it was too big.

'Don't worry, it'll cling ter yer when it's wet.'

We walked out of the cubicle together, but when I saw such an expanse of water I became nervous. I didn't even have the courage to go in the shallow end. I just sat on the side and was content to dangle my feet in the water, watching Winnie dive and swim in the deep end. But as I was sitting there someone came behind me and pushed me in. I panicked, went down like a brick, and hit the bottom. When I came up to the top, I almost choked. Foolishly, I began to clutch at the water, and went down a second time. The next thing I knew, I was being dragged towards the steps on the end of the pole. I then began to climb out. I didn't realise I was naked until I saw the attendant holding up what looked like a wet prehistoric bumblebee. I was overcome with shame. Putting one hand over my titties and the other to hide my private parts, I slid along the wet slabs to find the cubicle. In my confusion I turned into the wrong one. Someone swung the door out again, and I almost landed in the water once more. But Winnie came to the rescue and dragged me along into the next one.

She collected the 'bumblebee' while I dried and got dressed, and when she came back, she told me who it was that had pushed me in.

'Don't cry now,' she said. 'I'll push 'er in next week, an' 'old 'er down! Until she apologises ter yer,' she added.

'But I ain't comin' again,' I whimpered.

'Yer'll enjoy it when once yer've learnt ter swim.'

'I'll never learn, anyway I ain't wearin' that monstrosity again,' I said, throwing it on the floor.

'Well, will yer come an' watch me? Yer needn't get undressed.'

I agreed, but it was no fun just watching, and I was so eager to learn. A couple of weeks later, I told my dad that I wanted to learn to swim.

'All the other girls in our class go, Dad, but I ain't got a costume.'

'Well, if that's all that's worryin' yer, I'll buy yer one from the second-'and market.'

Sure enough, he bought me one which was made of some kind

of black woollen material, with white polka dots and frills around
the neck and the bottom of the skirt, and a cap to match. And
they fitted. I threw my arms around his neck and thanked him.
But when Mum saw it she said, ''ow much did that cost yer?'

'Only 'alf a crown,' he replied.

'I could 'ave bought food with that, instead of turnin' 'er 'ead
on such silly folderols!'

He told her it was his baccy money he'd saved, and that I
wanted to learn to swim. I remember she just shrugged her
shoulders and walked out.

I thought, whatever happens, I'll pay him back for his
kindness. I was now determined I was going to be the swimmer
my Dad would be proud of. And so I made a nuisance of myself,
pestering the attendant to teach me, at first with the pole. A few
weeks later, I won my certificate for ten lengths of the bath. And
I was very happy to see how proud my dad was of me, as he hung
it on the wall next to my brothers' twenty-length certificates. In
the coming weeks I became a better swimmer than Winnie. I
even learned to dive, and I won my next certificate for twenty
lengths.

But I was also determined that, whatever happened, I would
manage to give my dad his half-crown back. He was still out of
work, and it upset me when I used to see him splitting open nub
ends of cigarettes for tobacco to put in his clay pipe.

Winnie was very kind, and each time we ran errands we saved
our halfpennies. But this way it was taking too long for me to save
the half-crown *and* the coppers to go swimming. Then one day, as
we were walking along the Parade, we saw workmen digging up
the tar blocks from between the tram lines. Winnie went up to
one and asked if we could have some.

'No, yow can't! Bugger off, before I clout yer ear'oles!' he
shouted. But we weren't to be put off. We hid ourselves and
waited until the workmen moved further along the tram lines,
then we came from our hiding place and helped ourselves to
several blocks that we saw stacked up against the wall. These we
sold, two for a penny and no questions asked, to some of the poor
people several streets away, who couldn't afford threepence for a

bag of coal, or a bucket of slack. We thought we could help ourselves regularly, but other people must have had the same idea. The next day the rest had been carted away.

Another afternoon I did a very foolish and wicked thing. My eldest sister, Mary, had come to visit my mum. As I sat on the stool by the fire I heard them having high words. Mum wanted Mary to lend her some money, but Mary was adamant. 'No! You've had the last off me. I never get it back.' In her temper she bounced out, with Mum following her. I noticed Mary had forgotten to pick up her purse, which was lying on the table. Quickly I opened it to look inside, and when I saw some loose change, including two half-crowns, temptation got the better of me. I took out one half-crown and closed the purse. Almost immediately I wanted to put it back, but it was too late, my sister had come back for the purse, and left again with it.

Now I was scared. As soon as I thought about it I knew I couldn't really give the half-crown to my dad, he'd ask questions where I got it from, and I couldn't ever lie to him – he always had a way of finding out. I would have to try to return it somehow. There was only one answer. When Mary called again, I'd try and slip it into her purse, or drop it in her coat pocket. Meanwhile I hid it inside one of my woollen stockings. I even went to sleep in my stockings, in case I lost the half-crown. The coin seemed to burn a hole in my leg with guilt.

Mary called again the next day, and as soon as I saw her, I went hot. She must have seen guilt written all over me.

'Katie,' she said at once, 'after I left my purse here yesterday, there was half a crown missing. Did you take it?'

I hid my face in my hands and began to sob.

She shook me several times. 'You little thief! I've a good mind to tell yer dad. Where is it?'

'It's down me stockin',' I managed to whimper. 'I'm ever so sorry, Mary, I won't do it again.'

'You won't get the chance! Anyhow, why did you take it?'

Between sobs I told her how Dad had gone without his baccy to buy me my swimming costume, and I wanted to pay him back.

'You little fool! Stealing isn't the answer!' she said. 'You know you can pay him back in other ways. He told me how proud he was when you won your certificates. That was payment enough. And remember he doesn't go short of a smoke when I'm about . . . Do you understand what I've been telling you?'

'Yes,' I managed to answer.

'Now, dry yer eyes before Mum comes in, you know how she'll belt you if she finds out. But if you'll promise not to steal again, I'll not tell Mum, or Dad.'

I promised. But for months, each time she came to visit us, I always coloured up, still feeling ashamed to look at her.

3

Hard Times and Good Times

As far back as I can remember, when I was a child, there was always hardship and unemployment. I knew many a man spend his days from dawn till dusk searching for any kind of odd jobs that would bring in a few pennies to help feed a young family. And many a woman had to leave her children to roam the streets while she went out scrubbing someone else's house. In their desperation and despair, people would take on anything.

During one very cold spell, everyone in the yard was burning any kind of rubbish on the fire, to keep warm, or to cook. My dad chopped up the shutters from outside the window, which were hanging off anyway. And the neighbours followed suit. Mum, one afternoon, said I would have to take a sack and gather some branches that had blown off the trees down the lanes.

I called for Winnie and off we went. When we got as far as Wasson Pool, we could see other kids had been before us. We walked miles to try to fill that sack, until we came to a canal where there were more trees with low branches. As we went towards them we saw a flat hand-cart with a sack like ours strewn across it, and two men with their backs towards us, stripping off their clothes. At first glance we thought they'd come here to settle some argument, which we had often seen men do, but when we saw them strip themselves naked, we became scared, so we hid ourselves behind a large tree.

''ush,' Winnie whispered, 'don't move, or mek a sound. We'll afta wait 'ere now, till they go.'

'What they goin' ter do?' I whispered back.

'I don't know, we'll afta wait an' see.'

I didn't want to wait. I'd never seen any men naked before, and I was afraid and ashamed.

'Not me, Winnie, I'm off,' I said.

But before I could move one step, she pulled me down into the long grass beside her.

'Keep quiet,' she said. 'We can't go now, they'll 'ear us, an' yer know what that'll mean.'

I knew well enough. I didn't fancy a beating, or being tossed into that dirty, oily canal. Suddenly, we heard one of the men say, 'I think I 'eard some bugger movin' about out theea, Joe,' pointing towards where we were hiding. We became really scared.

'Don't be bleedin' daft,' was the other's reply.

'Well, I 'eard summat, do yer think it could be the rossers?'

'It can't be, they'd 'av arrested us afower now, so come on. It's about time fer the other two ter come up.'

All of a sudden there was a splash, as two more naked men rose up out of the water, each carrying a large lump of coal. When we saw who they were, we couldn't believe our eyes.

It was Winnie's father, and my dad.

We had to stay there now, and watch as the other two men dived in. This went on for about fifteen minutes, until the sack was full. After drying themselves down with their shirts, they put the sack of coal on the cart, and quickly dressed and away they went.

As soon as we felt safe to come out from our hiding place, we picked up our half-empty sack and began to laugh out loud.

'That was a near escape,' I giggled.

'Yes, an' did yer see what was danglin'?'

We tittered all the way home. But when we got to the end of our street and I said we'd meet the next day, she replied, 'Can't see yer termorra, Katie. I'll afta go ter confession.'

'What for?' I asked, as she tittered again.

'Well, yer know it was wrong fer us ter watch them naked bodies.'

'But we couldn't 'elp it.'

'I know, but I won't feel clean again, until I go.'

'Are you a Catholic then, Winnie?' I asked.

'No. Me and our Willie was born in Tipton. So was me dad. But me mum's Irish, and she's a Catholic, but she never goes ter Mass, she always ses *she* knows what's wrong, an' what's right, without bein' an' 'ypocrite.'

'But why do *yow* go? Is the priest nice lookin'?'

'Ooh no, 'e's quite ugly and shifty-eyed, and 'as a big purple bulbous nose, that sticks out like a ripe plum, ready ter burst. An' 'e drinks whiskey.'

''Ow do yer know that?' I asked.

''e come round to see me mum one day an' only me and me dad was in, and when me dad offered 'im a drop of Scotch, 'e said 'e only drank Irish. But 'e wasn't fussy the next day when 'e come an' me dad gave 'im some Scotch.'

'An' what do yer say when yer go ter confessional?'

'Well, when I go inter the box, 'e always seems to be waitin' fer me, an' 'e ses, "I see it's you again, and what have you to tell me this time?" When I tell 'im, 'e give me a kind of a lecture, then tells me I'm forgiven. So yer see it's easy when yer do things wrong, yer can start again after yer've been forgiven. See what I mean?'

No, I didn't see what she meant, but I nodded my head and said I'd call for her sometime.

When I got indoors, the first thing I noticed was a roaring coal fire, which I hadn't seen for years. Dad was naked apart from his trousers, with his bare feet resting on the fender, sitting in front of the fire, while Mum was drying his wet shirt on the back of the chair.

When I gave Mum the half-sack of twigs, he suddenly turned around. 'An' where 'ave yer bin till now?' he asked.

'Gettin' some broken branches fer Mum,' I replied nervously.

'I dain't ask yer what yer got!' he snapped. 'I asked yer where yer'd bin.'

I nearly blurted out 'by the canal', but checking myself in time I quickly said, 'By the . . . Wasson Pool.'

Just then Mum piped up. 'Yer better get yer 'ands washed and 'ave yer tea.'

I sat up at the table, but each mouthful I took I kept glancing
up at Dad's bare back, thinking perhaps he already knew Winnie
and I were there that afternoon, watching him in his nakedness.
And each time he happened to glance across at me I felt guilty
and ashamed.

Mum left the table to put more coal on the fire, but Dad
suddenly yelled out: 'I dain't get nearly drowned fer yow ter waste
it! Any'ow, yow'll afta go steady with it. I won't be able to go
again fer some time.'

'Why?' she asked.

'Why? Because I *can't* go again, till there's nobody about.
That's why. And Joe said somebody 'ad bin watchin' us this
afternoon.'

'Ooh dear, who was it?' Mum asked.

'I don't know, it worn't the cops. Joe said it must 'ave bin some
kids playing about. An' I don't want 'er goin' near that canal,' he
replied, pointing his finger at me.

I went all hot. Did he really suspect me? Was he waiting for me
to explain? Please, God, I prayed to myself, don't ever let him
find out it was Winnie and me.

A week later Dad tried his luck again with Mr Nashe, but they
came back with an empty sack, telling Mum it was too dangerous
now, a man and a woman had been arrested.

Next time Winnie and me met, we quarrelled. She asked me if
I would go along the canal again with her.

'No! I don't! I don't want ter go near it again, never,' I
snapped.

'Why?'

'Because I think it's wrong an' dirty.'

'Oh, please yerself,' she snapped.

'An' I think my dad suspects me.'

''ow could 'e, *my* dad never said anything.'

'Any'ow, yow betta not go near again. The bobbies 'ave
already arrested a man and a woman,' I said.

'Yes, I know, I saw 'em.'

'Yer saw 'em? When?'

'A few days ago.'

'Anybody we know?' I asked.

'Yes, it was Mr and Mrs Carter, from out of Sloane Street.'

'Oh dear. Ain't that the woman yer sold a rug to?'

'Yes.'

'Are yer sure it was them?' I asked.

'I went along the canal one afternoon with our Willie, when we saw Mr Carter strip an' jump in the water. While 'is wife was on the look-out, the cops came. She tried to warn 'im by shoutin' inter the water, but it was too late. When 'e come up, they were both arrested. Me an' Willie tried ter warn 'em, but we were too late. Any'ow we 'ad ter run an' 'ide ourselves, or they would 'ave arrested *us*.'

Listening to all this made me feel sick, for she seemed to be enjoying telling me. Suddenly I screamed at her, 'I think you're wicked, Winnie Nashe, an' Willie, ter go there ter watch naked men again. I suppose you'll go in the confessional box again too, an' ask the priest ter forgive yer again, so yer can do somethin' else yer know what's wrong . . . Yer know what yow are? . . . Winnie . . . bloody . . . Nashe . . . a bloody 'ypocrite! An' I never want ter speak to yer ever again!' I yelled.

And there I left her, standing with her mouth wide open gawping at me. We passed each other by like strangers for the next few days. A week later I said I was sorry, and we made it up.

*

During that year, my dad and Mr Nashe were the best of mates. They went everywhere together to look for work. People often used to turn and stare when Mr Nashe tried to keep up a pace with my dad. Often I thought, how comical. He was such a little man, where my dad was six foot tall and as strong as an ox; no one ever got the best of an argument when Dad was around.

Early one morning Mr Nashe called to tell Dad that there was a couple of porters wanted on Snow Hill railway station. Dad left a note on the table to tell Mum he'd be back soon. She waited all day, but when he returned she was pleased to hear that Mr Nashe and he had got the jobs as porters. He said it was only temporary until something better could be found. But it was better than being on parish relief.

He worked all hours, and the few coppers that passengers sometimes gave him when he carried their bags helped to give Mum a bit extra, which pleased her enormously. Each night he came home tired and dirty. But although we were very poor, Dad was a proud man. The clothes he wore were well patched, but he always kept himself clean. Each night, no matter how late, before he sat down to eat, he would strip to the waist and wash himself down, and if it wasn't too late, Mum would let me wait up and get his bowl of water ready to wash his tired, swollen feet.

In the middle of September we heard there was a fair at the Serpentine grounds in Aston (I think it was called the Onion Fair). The following Saturday I heard Dad ask Mum if she would like to go.

'Not me,' she replied. 'I've got too much to do. Any'ow, I don't know why yer want ter waste yer money on that place, it's only a catchpenny.'

'Can I go, Mum?' I asked eagerly.

'No, yer can't. I want yer ter fetch me half 'undredweight o' coal from the wharf.'

'Can I go Dad, when I come back?' I pleaded.

'No, yow 'eard what yer Mum said.'

'But Winnie's goin' with 'er dad,' I replied.

'I don't care who Winnie's goin' with, yow ain't goin', an' that's that. An' I've told yer befower, yer know what I've promised yer if I see yer with 'er again.'

But I did go.

As I was wheeling the coal trolley from the wharf, I happened to meet Winnie.

'Yer goin' ter the fair, Katie?' were her first words.

'No, me mum and dad said I wasn't ter go.'

'But I'm goin', why don't yer come with me?'

'I daren't, your dad'll tell my dad, and I'd get in trouble.'

'My dad ain't takin' me, 'e said I'd gorra stop an' 'elp Mum, but Mum said I could go as long as me dad dain't see me there.'

'Yer sure 'e won't see yer?' I asked.

'O' course 'e won't, they'll be crowds of people there, so 'e won't be able to see us if we look out.'

'Are yer sure it's safe ter go?' I asked.

'O' course I am, an' I've got a whole shillin' I've saved, an' we'll share it. See you two o'clock,' she added.

I was tempted, and I said that I'd do my best to meet her. But she was not to wait after a quarter past two, in case I couldn't make it.

After returning the trolley and giving back the penny deposit off the trolley to Mum, I asked if I could go out and play.

'No, yer can't!' she yelled. 'Yer betta light the candle, I want yer ter come with me down the cellar ter fetch up some slack fer the brew'ouse fire.'

We went down and I held the lighted candle while she sorted over slack and whatever rubbish she could burn under the boiler. I kept wondering how I could get away to meet Winnie. But Mum made it easy for me. As soon as we came up the cellar again, she said she didn't feel well and was going to lie down on the bed.

'Leave the bucket in the pantry an' don't mek a racket,' she said. 'An' tell yer dad ter wake me up when 'e comes in.'

Now was my chance. Should I ask again? Or should I just go, and not ask? But what if she refused, and found me another job to do? No. I'll go now, and suffer the consequences later. It was after two o'clock when I met Winnie. She told me she was just about to go without me. I was glad she'd waited.

'Come on, 'urry up,' she called out, grabbing my hand.

As we hurried along, I asked, ''ave yer been to a fair befower?'

'Yes, lots of times with me mum and dad, but not this one. An' it'll be better and more fun without them.'

'Why?' I asked.

'Well, we can go all over the place an' do what we want ter do.'

'I hope me dad, or your dad, won't see us.'

''e won't see yer if yer keep by me. Now come on an' stop yer worryin'.'

'All right, I'll try.'

I'd never been inside a fairground before. The music and the noise from the crowds of people of all ages was quite deafening, and as soon as we mingled with the crowd I lost my nervousness and began to enjoy the merriment. Winnie shared her shilling and we bought candy floss and popcorn. Then we tried to win a goldfish, but we had no luck, and Winnie said it was a catchpenny. Then we went on the swings. Now we only had tuppence each left.

'What shall we buy now?' I asked.

'Come on,' she said. 'Yer see that coconut shy over there? Well, let's 'ave a go at that.'

But as we stood there making up our minds, the big fellow who stood beside the stall shouted out at us.

'What yow two kids starin' at? Bugger off.'

'Walk up, walk up, three balls a penny,' he kept repeating. Then, 'If yer don't clear off, I'll put me foot be'ind yer.'

'But we want ter 'ave a go,' Winnie said.

'Yer gotcha money?' he snapped.

We both held our hands out, and showed him our last tuppences. He quickly helped himself to them and gave us three balls each. Winnie threw hers, and I thought I had to throw mine at the same time.

'Yer don't throw 'em together,' he bawled out. 'Yer throw 'em one at a time!'

He gave us the other three each and we tried again. But we walked away disappointed. We had no money left now, and we were hungry, dirty and disheartened, so we decided we'd go home. But when we saw and heard a crowd laughing and jeering, we stopped to see what it was all about. We managed to squeeze through the crowd and had full view of a crude open air boxing ring, with sawdust on the floor. Inside the ring were the prize fighter and his manager. The manager was calling out, 'Who dares ter come inter the ring ter pay 'alf a crown and win a golden sovereign?'

It frightened me even to look at the boxer with his nose flattened across his face, two red cauliflower ears, and thick lips. He was leaping backwards and forwards, and each time he came towards the ropes he waved his arms like some wild beast. 'Yow,

yow! Yow! Or yow!' He kept pointing to the men, but no one would take up the challenge.

'Only three rounds and yer can win yerself a sovereign, *and* yer 'alf-crown back,' the manager kept calling out.

Winnie and I were about to move on away, when suddenly we heard a familiar voice say, 'Go on Sam, yow've done some fightin' in the Army. Yow can beat 'im.'

When we looked among the crowd, we saw it was our dads.

I didn't know whether to stay or run, but Winnie wanted to stay and see what was going to happen. So I had to stay too, hoping my dad wouldn't see me.

'Go on Sam,' I heard Mr Nashe repeat again. 'Yow can do *ten* rounds with 'im, let alone three.'

'Well, I could do with the money, but I ain't even got the price of a pint, let alone 'alf a crown.'

'I'll lend it yer, Sam, an' yer can pay me back when yer win.'

I heard the crowd cheering for Dad to take up the challenge. I felt now I had to stay and watch, and pray that he would win. But I was alarmed when someone called out, 'Yow don't wanta go in theea, mate, 'e'll slaughter yer.'

'I couldn't stand one round, an' it was me last 'alf-crown,' came from another man at the back.

But admist the cheers of the rest, Dad went beneath the rope. Almost before he could enter the ring the bruiser made a dive, but Dad was too quick for him and ducked. He swung again before he could strip off his shirt, but again Dad sidestepped, and as the bruiser stumbled there were cheers from all sides. Crowds of people from the stalls now came to watch the fight.

As soon as the first round was over I looked among the crowd for Winnie. When I saw her talking to her dad I got scared. I was about to run from the crowd when I felt Winnie pull me back.

'Yer don't 'ave ter go now, me dad's told me ter fetch yer where we can get a betta view.'

'But me dad'll see me.'

'O' course 'e won't, 'e'll be too busy fightin'. Now come on an' don't look so scared.'

'Mr Nashe,' I said, 'please don't tell me dad I've been 'ere.'

'Well, yer betta keep quiet if yer wanta stay.'

'Do yer think me dad'll win?' I asked.

'O' course 'e'll win, luv, an' when it's over yer betta 'urry off 'ome, the pair o' yer.'

The second round was now about to start. And as soon as the bruiser's manager (or rather, owner, trainer and referee, all rolled into one) rang the bell, Dad was on his feet.

'Come on yer bloody big ape,' he called out with his fists at the ready.

Dad landed heavy blows to the boxer's body. The bruiser, when he got closer, put his two long hairy arms around Dad and nearly threw him down on the wet sawdust. But when Dad managed to break loose, he caught the boxer a blow to his chin, and down he went. The cheers from the crowds were quite deafening. I was getting excited too. Suddenly the fighter's trainer threw a bucket of dirty water all over him. 'Get up, yer bleedin' fool. If yer lay there yer'll know what ter expect!' he yelled.

As he staggered to his feet the bell went. That was supposed to be the end of the round, but the crowd thought different. They hissed and booed, shouting that there was another minute to go. Everyone standing there knew Dad had beaten the fighter. When the third round began there were more cheers for Dad. I was now enjoying watching.

'Come on, matey!' someone shouted out. 'Yow can beat 'im. Keep away from 'is clutches.'

'We'll see yer get fair play,' others yelled out.

But Dad was not having it all his own way. When the bruiser landed Dad another blow, and I saw blood coming from his mouth, I went wild. Forgetting where I was, I shouted, 'Yer bleedin' varmint!'

Dad was startled by my voice and gave me a quick glance, and the bruiser, seeing his chance, gave Dad another blow, which put him flat on his back.

The referee didn't bother to count. Raising bruiser's hand, he declared him the winner. But by this time Dad had sprung to his feet and as the boxer was taking his bow, Dad gave him an uppercut that laid him flat out. The manager hurled another bucket of water over him, but when that had no effect he had to begin counting him out, very slowly.

At first the manager refused to pay out, saying the fight hadn't gone the full three rounds. But when the crowd said they would lynch him, he soon gave Dad the gold sovereign and the half-crown. I didn't wait for Dad to put on his shirt, I ran and hid among the crowd, but he soon found me. I burst out crying. I believe he would have hit me there and then if Winnie and her dad hadn't come on the scene. Pulling me towards him, he asked why I was there, but before I could manage to blurt out why, Winnie said, 'It's my fault, she didn't wanta come.'

'All right, but what I wanta know is, 'ow long 'ave yer bin swearin'?'

'I don't say it, Dad, only when I get mad, but I'm always 'earing Mum say it.'

'All right, wipe yer eyes an' yer can 'ave a tanner each ter spend on the stalls. When yer've spent that, yer can meet me an' Joe by the coconut shy.'

So off Winnie and me skipped, but instead of going to the stalls we had several rides on the roundabouts. Then we went back to the coconut shy to meet our dads. There we saw them trying their luck. Mr Nashe had already won a teddy bear for Winnie, and Dad was trying his best to win one for me, but no luck. It was then, when I looked up at him, that I saw his right eye was swollen, and almost closed. And a front tooth was missing. My own eyes filled with tears.

'I'm sorry, Dad,' I blurted out.

'It's me that's sorry, luv. I'll buy yer one next week.'

'I don't want one, Dad,' I whimpered. 'I said I was sorry because it was my fault. If I 'adn't 'ave shouted, an' swore when I did, you wouldn't 'ave been 'urt.'

'I was 'urt before I 'eard or saw yer, luv. Now, dry yer eyes an' you an' Winnie betta get off 'ome now, before it gets dark.'

'Dad, yer won't tell Mum I was at the fair, will yer?' I asked.

'Why? Don't she know?'

'She said she didn't feel well an' went ter lie down, an' I was to tell yer when yer come in ter wake 'er up. Then I went with Winnie.'

'Where's Winnie now?'

'Over there, with 'er dad,' I answered, pointing to one of the stalls.

'We'd betta go over to 'em, then yer betta get off 'ome.'

'Dad, please don't tell Mum I was at the fair, will yer?' I repeated.

'Not unless she asks me . . . But if she asks *you* yer must tell 'er the truth. Do yer understand? I won't be long after you,' he added.

'Yes, Dad,' I replied.

Winnie and I hurried home from the fair. When I got indoors I was glad to see that Mum was still upstairs. The fire was nearly out, but I set to, put some coal on, and hurried it along with the bellows. Then I set to tidy up the room, and to lay the table ready for Dad coming in.

'Is yer Mum still upstairs?' he asked as soon as he entered.

'Yes,' I answered.

'Come an' see what I bought 'er.'

He put his hand inside his waistcoat pocket and pulled out a small green cardboard box. Inside was a large gilt cameo brooch about the size of a half-crown.

'Nice, ain't it?' he said.

'Yes, that'll please 'er,' I said.

When she came downstairs and saw Dad's face, she yelled, 'Oh my God! What yer done ter yerself?'

'It's a long story, Polly, but first let me show yer what I've bought yer.'

As soon as she saw the gilt brooch, sure enough, her eyes lit up.

'Is it gold?' she asked.

'Well . . . it's near enough, but don't try an' pawn it.'

'Oh, no, Sam. I'll just wear it on me birthday.' (But knowing my Mum, I was sure she'd try to pawn it some day.)

I watched as she put it back in its box then dropped it in the vase on the mantleshelf, among the pawn tickets.

While we were eating, Mum noticed the gap in Dad's mouth.

'Where's yer tooth?' she asked.

'I don't know, Polly, I think I must 'ave swallowed it,' he replied, winking at me.

All that afternoon and evening, I was on thorns, wondering whether she would ask me any questions. But she never did. I believe she was too pleased about her present to question me.

Later, I asked my dad if he really had bought that cameo brooch.

'Why do yer ask?' he said.

When I told him I'd seen two or three like it at the fair, he said, 'Well luv, I tried ter win it, 'cause I knew yer mum would like it, an' when I did win it, I realised it cost me more than it was worth.'

'It's very pretty, Dad. Is it gold?' I asked.

'No luv, it's only gilt,' he replied.

A few weeks after that, as I was sitting on the wooden sofa, trying to finish knitting a scarf for my brother from odd scraps of wool, I saw my mum's eyes kept looking up at the mantleshelf.

Now, if ever she wanted anything, it was always me. 'Fetch this! Fetch me that!' Even when things were near at hand.

'Yer betta stand on the stool and reach me down that purse,' she said.

As soon as I saw her face, I knew she had found it was empty. And when she told me to reach down the vase and take out the little green cardboard box, I knew at once what she was going to do. She slipped on Dad's cap and put the box into her apron pocket. I said, 'Dad said yer wasn't ter pawn it.'

'Yer Dad won't know, an' I'm warnin' yer if yer dare tell 'im, yer know what ter expect.'

'Any 'ow,' she added, 'I've gorra buy summat to eat. I'll be able to get it back on Saturday. And yer can come with me an' call at the butcher's on the way back.'

The pawn shop had once been a dwelling house and it was very small, with a narrow entry at the side, where neighbours queued up with their bundles of washing under their arms, or whatever else they could find to pawn. Over the entry were the three brass

balls and a rusty sign which read: S. J. Woolf, Pawnbroker. There
was only room for two people at a time in the shop, everyone else
had to stay in the entry until it was their turn.

My mum was called in at the same time as Mrs Ellis. Now, Mrs
Ellis was one of the neighbours in the next yard, and Mum didn't
like her. When Mum got near the counter, Mrs Ellis stared at her
in surprise.

'Yow fetchin' summat out?' she asked.

'What yow want ter know for?' Mum snapped.

'Well, I don't see yer carrin' any washin'.' She snapped back.

Mum took out the box from her apron pocket, and slapped it
down on the counter. 'Can yer lend me a couple of bob on this
till Saturday?' she said.

But when the pawnbroker opened the box, he almost threw it
back at her. 'This ain't no good to me, missus,' he snapped.

'Well,' Mum pleaded, 'lend me a shillin' on it. I'll fetch it back
on Saturday,' she added.

'No. It ain't even worth the box it stands in.'

Mum picked up the box and as she dropped it back into her
apron pocket she pushed past Mrs Ellis, almost knocking her
over. When we got out into the street, I saw tears in Mum's eyes
as she muttered, "er would be theea, now it'll be all over the
neighbourhood. But it'll be the last time I'll tek anything theea,
the old skinflint.'

As we hurried along Albion Street she said I was to call in the
butcher's. 'Ask 'im ter let me 'ave sixpennorth o' bits till
Friday . . . I'll slip 'ome an' put the kettle on,' she said.

'I don't like to, Mum, 'e refused me last time. 'e said you owed
enough for one week,' I replied.

'Oh, well, yer better go in an' ask 'im fer some lights for the
cats.'

'But we've only one cat, Mum,' I said.

'Well, if yer say cats, 'e'll p'raps give yer mower. Now, 'urry
yerself,' she snapped. 'I ain't got all day.'

When I went in to the butcher's, he just stared. 'If yer've come
fer meat, tell yer mother she'll 'ave ter come 'erself, and pay a bit
off what she already owes,' he said.

'I 'aven't come fer meat, Mr Underwood. Mum sent me fer some lights fer the cats.'

''ow many cats 'ave yer got?'

'Only one, but Mum shares it out to the neighbours' cats,' I pleaded.

'Very well,' he replied. 'But don't forget, I want ter see yer mother on Friday.'

As soon as I had thanked him for the lights I ran all the way home. When I got indoors I gave Mum his message, but she just shrugged her shoulders. I asked if I should put the brooch back in the vase, but she said she had already done it.

In those days, I often had to fetch a pennyworth of jam in a cup, or a pennyworth of dripping from Stoddard's, the pork butcher's at the corner of Icknield Street. 'An' don't forget ter tell 'im ter put plenty of dark jelly with it,' she would say. It was always a pennyworth of this, or that.

Each Saturday morning, my mum would send us to Houghton's, the butcher's in Broad Street. He was very kind to us kids, and always gave a little extra meat with our small order. Sometimes we'd take the little kids from our yard and give them a ride in the go-cart. Sometimes we went the long way round, down Camden Drive, along Arthur Place, down the Sandpits, then up Nelson Street. The reason was, there was a large fruit, vegetable and fish stall on the corner of Nelson Street, and the owner was another person who was kind to us. Whenever he saw us passing that way he would call us over, and put some bruised fruit, or a haddock, or a few herrings, in our cart. 'Cover 'em over an' take 'em straight 'ome to yer mum,' he'd say.

Sometimes, when he wasn't about, we'd carry on along Vincent Street, along Sheepcote Street, along the narrow passage called King Edward Place, and across the horse road to Houghton's. But before we crossed the horse road, we used to linger on the corner of the narrow passageway, where there was an ice cream parlour (I think the name was Devotis), hoping that someone would be kind enough to give us an ice cream, even if it was only a lick. But we were always shooed away.

When we called at the butcher's, it was always sixpennyworth of pieces. Sometimes he'd give us a large piece of hipbone steak, which had fallen off the chopping block into the sawdust, or a couple of pork chops and a breast of lamb. Or sometimes there'd be pork bones and a piece of belly draft. All of which Mum had to swill well to get the sawdust off. But she was always pleased when she saw what we'd bought for sixpence.

But one such Saturday, as we wheeled the little cart towards the ice cream parlour, I saw my brother Frankie take out a cracked cup from under the sack. When I asked him what it was for, he said, 'Don't ask questions, we're goin' in fer a pennorth of ice cream.'

'Not me,' I said. "e'll only run us out. I'll wait on the corner.'

Soon he came out of the shop, grinning all over his face.

'Come on,' he cried out, 'before I eat it all meself.'

As we were taking turns scooping it out with our fingers, I asked him where he'd got the penny from.

'I ain't tellin'! Now, come on an' let's fetch the meat,' he snapped.

As soon as the cup was empty he hid it under the sack again.

We wheeled the little cart inside the butcher's, and as my brother stood against the counter I heard him say, 'Please, Mr 'oughton, me mum ses, can yer let 'er 'ave five pennorth today?'

I knew then he had used one of the pennies for the ice cream.

As the butcher was wrapping up our five pennyworth, I saw Frankie knock two udders off the end of the counter into the cart, covering them over with the sack. I was dumbstruck and scared, for I'd never known him to do anything like this before. Then, when we had received our parcel of meat and were on our way, I said, 'Frankie, you shouldn't 'ave done that. If Mum finds out, she'll skin yer alive.'

'Why? Yer goin' to tell 'er then? If yer do, yer'll know what to expect!'

Of course, I had no intention of telling Mum. But as soon as we got home and she saw what was in the parcel, she said, "e ain't gid yer much. I'll tell 'im when I see 'im.'

When Frankie handed Mum the two udders she was suspicious. 'Where did yer get them from?' she asked. 'An' look at 'em, covered with dirt.'

When he told her Mr Houghton had given them to him she didn't believe him. 'Yow'll tek 'em back this minute!' she yelled.

He was scared now, and ran off down the street. When she asked me if I knew anything about them, I lied. I said I didn't know until I saw them in the cart. But she wrapped them up in newspaper and almost dragged me back with her to the butcher's. I knew at once that he'd missed them, for as soon as we entered, he waved the chopper at us and yelled, 'If them little buggers come anywhere near my shop again, I'll chop their bloody 'ands off with this chopper!'

Mum made all the excuses she could think of, and when she handed over the udders to him, he said, 'Yer betta take 'em now, I won't be able to sell 'em like that. But I'm warnin' yer! Next time I see 'em, I'll put the bobbies on to 'em.'

When we got home Frankie was nowhere to be seen, but when he did come in, later that night, she gave him the biggest caning he'd ever had. She was also mad we had lost such a good kind butcher, and had to try elsewhere. But I noticed she was pleased to clean the udders, and prepare them for our meals.

I was glad too, that she never found out about how we managed to buy that ice cream. Otherwise, Frankie would have had another belting off Dad, and maybe I'd have had one too.

*

When Dad's job as a porter came to an end, he told us we would all have to put our shoulders to the wheel. My brother Jack was now the only one who was bringing home his small pittance. My eldest sister, Mary, was already married and had a home of her own. And my brother Charlie was living with his two friends Billy and Albert Wynn and their widowed mother – though he always sent home whatever he could spare. Frankie, Liza and me were still at school.

Dad began to chop and sell firewood again. Frankie and me had to help, while my sister Liza, often grumbling, helped Mum. In the winter, as soon as there was a promise of snow, Dad'd wake Frankie. Before it was daylight, I'd hear him call up the attic stairs, 'Come on, Frankie, it's goin' ter snow.' And I'd see my brother, half-awake, almost tumbling down the stairs, trying to get dressed as he went. With the shovel and the broom over their shoulders, they'd go from door to door, knocking and asking if people wanted their paths and the pavements outside their houses cleared. Sometimes they'd be out all night long. In the streets near us people might just give Dad a hot bowl of soup, or Frankie a drink of hot cocoa. If they couldn't afford even as much as that, Dad would sweep their paths for nothing. But when they went round the posher quarters (as Dad called them), he would get a shilling, or one and sixpence, for each path. When they came home, tired, wet and hungry, Dad would tip out his pockets. After giving Frankie sixpence, he'd count the rest out and give it to Mum. I remember one night he brought home over two pounds, and before he went up to bed he prayed the heavens would open up and send down snow more often. 'Meks a bloody good business. Betta than workin' in a factory,' he'd say.

We weren't always little drudges, sometimes we had great treats, such as a ride along the canal. We called it 'up the cut in the coal boat'. And though we had no toys to speak of, we had plenty of fun with games like hopscotch, marbles and jackstones.

But the best time of all was bonfire night. At this time of year, everyone who could afford it would get a new straw mattress. You would hear the 'Pat Man' coming down the hill with his cart.

'Come an' get a clean straw mattress,' he'd call out. 'A bob each, or two fer one an' ninepence. Three fer 'alf a crown.'

The old mattresses went on the bonfires there were in almost every yard on the Fifth of November. People would throw their bedroom or attic windows wide, and mattresses would come flying through the air. You'd be lucky if you saw them in time to duck. We children would help drag them to the end of the yard, where, with other rubbish, they'd be piled high, ready to be lit when it was dark. We'd also go around with a go-cart, or a coal trolley, and collect whatever rubbish we could find, or beg – old boxes, old stools, old palings, anything that would burn. And, of course, we'd beg pennies for the guy, to buy sparklers or Catherine wheels. The bonfire was lit as soon as it was dark, and there'd be singing and dancing round the fire till the early hours of the morning. For us young ones there'd be baked chestnuts and baked potatoes, half-raw and with the skins burnt black, but we were glad to eat them. The grown-ups had gallon stone jars of beer.

And then, if you were lucky, there was for once in a way a clean straw mattress to sleep on.

4

War, Work and Workmates

When war broke out in 1914, life changed for us all. My brothers Jack and Charlie joined up at once, without waiting for their call-up papers. Even Dad tried to enlist, but he failed his medical. Instead he got a job in a brass-casting shop, making shell cases. My sister Liza too got a job on munitions. There was plenty of war work for everyone, no scratching for pennies now.

I, too, yearned to leave school and be a grown-up woman, earning my own living. I shall never forget the day I left school. I was just fourteen. I hurried home all excited, feeling as free as a bird, and as I ran in the house I began to dance around the table. 'Rah, rah, rah!' I kept singing, 'Me schooldays are over, rah, rah, rah!'

My dad came and grabbed hold of me. ''old yer 'orses! 'ave yer gone mad, of a sudden?'

'No, Dad,' I replied. 'But I've said goodbye ter school terday, fer ever.'

'Well, yer betta tek yer pinny off, an' come an' sit on this chair, I want to talk ter yer, afower yer mum comes 'ome,' he said sternly.

'What 'ave I done now?' I asked.

'It's not what yer've done, it's what yer goin' ter do, luv,' he said more kindly.

'Yes, Dad,' I replied, as I sat facing him.

'Now, I want yer ter listen carefully, and remember what I'm goin' to say.'

'Yes, Dad,' I replied, and added quickly, all in one breath,

'Yes, Dad, an' I'm goin' ter work in a munition factory an' earn some money for you an' Mum.'

'That can wait, luv. What I want to say is this. Yer ter start work next Monday mornin'. Now, remember this, when yer work in a factory, it'll be strange ter yer at first, it'll be like another world. Yer'll be mixin' an' workin' with all kinds of older men and women, boys too. Now, if yer ever get into any difficulties, or want ter know anything, I want yer always to come and tell me, or yer mum, first.'

'Yes, Dad, but nobody seems ter know I'm growin' up, an' there's lots of things I want ter know.'

'Well, what's troublin' yer?' he asked.

'I want ter know about marriage, an' love, an' babbies, but when I ask Mum about these things, she gets angry with me an' yells it's not right fer me to even mention these things yet.'

'She's probably right, Katie, but she'll tell yer sometime. But don't try ter grow up too soon, luv,' he added. 'Yer too young yet ter understand lots of things.'

'But I think I know about love, because I love yow, Dad.'

'I love yow too, Katie,' he said gently. 'But there are lots of other kinds of loves, which yer'll understand more as yer grow older. Any'ow, I'll 'ave a talk with yer sister an' ask 'er if she'll explain these things ter yer.'

I threw my arms around his neck, and as I hugged and kissed him, he said again, 'Remember what I say, luv. Don't grow up too soon.'

But I didn't see my eldest sister for months. Her husband was also in the Army, somewhere in the country where she had the chance to visit him several times before he went abroad. By the time I did see her, I had almost forgotten Dad's warning.

My first job was working a metal press, cutting out brass buttons for army uniforms. But I didn't think I was paid enough for the hours and the hard work I did, so I soon left. In those first years I flitted several times from one job to another. Once I was working, although most of my wages went to Mum, I had enough money left to buy myself extra food, and some second-hand clothes. And my mother let me have more freedom now I was earning, and bringing home my wages each week.

One of my early jobs was working in a small press shop with four women of about my mother's age. These women were very coarse, and swore like troopers, but this didn't bother me. I was used to bad language at home, and from our neighbours in the yard.

At lunchtime the women sat on three-legged stools around the coke stove in the centre of the workshop, eating whatever food they had brought with them or, sometimes, fish and chips which they got me to fetch for them. When I had to go out to get the fish and chips I was always late going home for my own lunch. Using this as an excuse, I asked my mum if I too could have sandwiches to take, instead of coming home.

'Please yerself,' she said. 'But don't come back at nights sayin' yer 'ungry.'

So I stayed to have lunch with the women. I was pleased about this, mostly because I was dying to know what they talked about while they were sitting around the stove: I thought I might learn from them some of the things my mother wouldn't tell me. But whenever they saw me listening they would move closer to the stove, and lower their voices so I couldn't hear.

One lunchtime I was told to fetch their four tuppenny pieces of cod and four pennyworth of chips. 'An' 'urry yerself! We don't want 'em cold,' Florrie warned.

'We want 'em separate. An' put plenty of vinegar on,' Mabel called out as I hurried down the stairs.

But when I gave my order, and handed the money over the counter, the woman glared at me.

'Can't yer read?' she snapped, pointing to the notice on the wall.

As I turned around to read, she called out angrily, 'Cod's threepence now! An' chips are tuppence!'

'But I only 'ave a shillin', I replied. 'I'll 'ave ter go back an' tell 'em.'

'Who they for?' she asked.

When I told her, she said angrily, 'Don't they know there's a war on? Food's gettin' scarce, an' there's talk o' rationin'. Yow tell 'em they'll afta tighten their belts soon.'

But when I told them how much the fish and chips were, Florrie yelled, 'I don't believe yer. Yer little liar!'

Suddenly I flared up. 'Well! Yer can go yerself!' I shouted. 'If yer don't believe me. Anyway, yer'll 'ave ter tighten yer belts!' I added, throwing the shilling across the bench.

'Don't yer come 'ere with yer bloody cheek!' Mabel piped up, 'or I'll clout yer bleedin' ear'ole,' she added, raising her hand. But she picked up the shilling, and hurried to fetch the fish and chips herself.

She came back with nothing.

''er said they've got no fish left, an' the taters 'ave gone up,' Mabel said. 'Yer'll afta go an' try in Branston Street,' she told me.

'I'm not goin'. I ain't ate my sandwiches yet, an' it'll soon be time ter start ter work again,' I shouted back at the four of them. But I was ready to cry when she shouted in my ear, 'Yer'll do as yer told!'

Just then the foreman came in and when he heard what all the noise and commotion was about he said I was there to work, not to fetch and carry for them.

This didn't help matters. During the next few days, as usual, I tried to listen when they were whispering together. As soon as they saw me listening, Mabel called out, 'Yer'd betta get yer grub down yer, or yer'll get splinters in yer ears.'

'Yes, an' yer'll 'ear mower than wot's good fer yer one o' these days. Yer nosy, cheeky little sod!' Florrie added.

I dragged my stool further from the fire, but I still kept my ears cocked. I should have taken their warning. The next day, as we sat by the coke stove, I was surprised to find that they were talking loud enough for me to hear. Foolishly I listened, and innocently I believed every word they said.

'Fancy that! That's terrible!' I heard Mabel cry out.

'Wot's that yer talking about?' Alice asked.

'Don't yer know, Alice? All the other workers know,' Florrie replied.

Now I was all ears to know who they were talking about.

'Yer know that young girl as used ter work 'ere, 'er 'ad ter go ter the 'orspital,' Florrie said.

'Whatever for?' Alice asked.

'Well, she 'ad 'air growin' in between 'er legs.'

'Yer mean on 'er fanny?'

'Yes, an' if she don't get it cut off, it'll grow, an' grow, like an 'orse's tail, an' she'll be a freak,' Maggie piped up, looking at me.

I was too scared now to listen any more. I kicked over the stool and fled down the stairs as quick as I could go. I was terrified. I too had hair growing there. I didn't want to be a freak, or grow a horse's tail. But what was I going to do? For I was afraid of hospitals too.

When I got home I was relieved to find no one in. I flung myself down on the sofa and wept. There was no one I could confide in, least of all my mum. I thought there was only one thing to do, and I must do it quickly, before anyone came home. I couldn't lock the door, for the key had been lost years before. We didn't even have a knob on the old door, just the hole where it should have been. But I got some waste paper and plugged up the hole. Then I bolted the door and, taking the scissors Mum used for everything, I dropped my skirt, pulled down my drawers, and began to cut away the unwanted hair. But the scissors wouldn't cut butter hot, let alone my bum fluff. Suddenly I hit on using Dad's open razor from the table drawer. Just as I was about to make an attempt the door began to rattle. I started to tremble. The razor slipped and I cut myself. Quickly I threw the razor back inside the drawer, as the door rattled again.

'Who've yer got in theea? Open this dower at once! Befower I kick it down!' I heard my sister Liza yell. I unbolted the door, thinking how like my mum she sounded, as she yelled again, 'What yer got that dower locked for? Who've yer got in 'ere?' she added, as she looked around the room. 'I'm goin' ter tell Mum when she comes in.'

I couldn't speak. I just stood there, terrified at what I'd done. When she began to shake me, I stammered, 'Oh, Liza, I . . . I'm blee . . . bleedin' an' I . . . I'm scared.'

Before I could explain any more, she burst out laughing.

'That ain't nothin' ter be scared of. It's when yer don't see 'em, that's the time ter be scared,' she replied.

'It's not me monthlies, Liza,' I whimpered. 'I've cut meself with Dad's razor.'

'Yer done what? 'ow? Why?'

When I had managed to tell her why, she burst out laughing again. 'Yer bloody little fool, yow ain't a freak, everybody grows 'air theea, it's natural.'

When I said I didn't believe her, she stood up on the chair and brazenly pulled her skirt right up to her waist. She didn't have any drawers on.

'Look! If yer don't believe me!' she cried out, flaunting herself. 'I got a big bunch!'

Quickly I looked away. I felt ashamed to look, but I had to look again, before I could convince myself what I'd seen was true. When I took my eyes away, I was also curious to know why she wasn't wearing any bloomers.

'Why ain't yer wearin' any bloomers, Liza?' I asked.

'Oh, them?' she replied, as she jumped down off the chair. 'They're too much trouble ter pull down an' up.'

This didn't make any sense to me at the time.

'Come on, let's see what yer done,' she asked as she came towards me.

'No!' I yelled. 'It's not bleedin' now. It's stopped.'

I couldn't for the life of me show my nakedness to Liza.

'Please yerself,' she replied.

'Liza, I can't go back ter work at that place again,' I whimpered.

'Don't worry, I'll go an' collect yer wages, an' I'll mek some excuse ter yer gaffer. But it's worth a few coppers fer some fags,' she added.

'But what excuse am I goin' ter tell me mum?'

'Yow tell 'er nothin'. Just keep out of sight an' leave it ter me,' she replied.

'Promise yer won't tell her what's 'appened, Liza, yer know what 'er temper's like, she'll go ter that factory an' murder them women.'

'They'll very likely murder 'er, if they're like wot yow say they are,' she replied, smiling.

Although the bleeding had stopped, I felt very sore. After Liza left I bolted the door again, and reaching down some Fuller's Earth from the top cupboard, I sprinkled it between my legs. It felt easier for the moment, but when I sat down, I had to sit on the side of my bum.

'What's the matter with yow?' my mum yelled out, when she saw me trying to sit straight on the chair the following day.

'Noth . . . nothin', Mum,' I stammered.

'Yer gotta flea up yer arse or summat?'

'No, Mum,' I replied tearfully.

'Well, sit up straight, unless yer wanta grow up lopsided!'

'Yes Mum,' I replied painfully, as I tried.

'Any'ow, yer betta get the bass broom an' sweep outside the dower,' she added.

For once, I was grateful for her orders. I found it a relief to stand or walk about.

5

First Love

At the end of that week I had to dip down into my small savings to make my mum's money up. But I was grateful to Liza for keeping my secret – I hadn't really believed she would, for she often carried tales to my mother. I tried to buy her some Woodbines, which were scarce. There was talk now of food being rationed and, with more money to spend, people were also stocking up their cupboards in case of an invasion.

It was during the next week that I met my friend Winnie again, one evening as I was leaving my new job. I couldn't take my eyes off her. She'd grown into a pretty young woman, plump and shapely, but she'd dyed her red hair to blonde, which made her look older than her sixteen years. I was glad to see her again, and we got chatting at once.

I was surprised to find that she was working at the brass factory I had just left.

"ow long 'ave yer worked there?' I asked her.

'Two weeks,' she answered.

'That's funny, I never saw yer. But I left last week. Any'ow, what part of the factory do yer work in?'

'In the machine shop, on the ground floor, on a turnin' lathe, with some men and other girls. But the foreman's movin' me next week. I'm to work in another part fer more money.'

'You take a warnin' from me, Winnie, don't let 'im move yer inter that press shop!'

'Why?'

'That's where I used to work, with four coarse women, an' believe me Winnie, they're four real tykes.'

'Yer still a modest little miss, Katie, yer want ter tek life as it comes, like me. I don't care what people say or do. If I don't like what they say, it goes in one ear an' out the other. Any'ow, what's troublin' yer?'

'Come an' 'ave a cup of tea in the tea shop an' I'll tell yer all about it.'

It wasn't until I'd finished telling her all the things I'd done, that I saw the funny side. So did she. We both began to laugh out loud and almost choked on our tea.

I was really happy to have met her again. She was always fun to be with. But I was about to get into more trouble.

She said she had a young man to meet, from where she was working. 'Why don't yer come along, Katie? I'll introduce yer ter 'is friend,' she said.

'I don't know, Winnie. I've never been out with the opposite sex,' I replied.

'Yer don't 'ave ter to be nervous, or shy, 'e's quite a nice fellow. Any'ow, yer'll be all right. I won't leave yer. We'll make a foursome.'

She sounded convincing enough, so I agreed. I promised to meet her the following Saturday night at her mum's new address, in Edward Street, near the Sandpits.

I dolled myself up in a new satin blouse and long hobble skirt, and did my hair on top in a bun. With a dab of face powder and carmine on my cheeks, I felt the part of a grown-up miss. But when I was ready to go, I looked down at myself and noticed the neck of my blouse was too low, showing the top of my breasts. I thought of the cameo brooch my dad had won for my mum at the fair, I knew she always kept it in the vase, and I borrowed it to pin the top of my blouse together. When I arrived at Winnie's I was surprised to see the change in her mother. She looked much cleaner than I'd seen her before, when she used to make rag rugs for a living. Her red hair, which had always been untidy, was now well brushed and rolled into a bun at the back of her head, and she looked quite smart for such a dumpy little woman. As I stepped inside the room I noticed that that too was clean and tidy, and the table had a real white lace tablecloth spread with home-made buns, cakes, meat, even best butter and jars of different kinds of jams and pickles. Winnie's twin brother, Willie, was sitting with his feet up on the fender, smoking a cigar. As soon as Willie saw me, he said, "ello Kate, any chance of tekin' yer out fer a walk some night?'

Before I could reply his mother yelled out at him, 'No you can't! She's goin' out with a friend of Winnie's. An' take your feet down off that fender, before they come in.'

Trying to avoid looking at Willie, I concentrated on the display of food on the table. I wondered how Mrs Nashe had come by such an enormous amount of food, when everything was so short in the shops. I thought to myself, was she a hoarder? Or had she been lucky with some of the shopkeepers who had their own special customers? At this time, towards the end of 1918, most women were finding it very difficult to get enough to feed their families. Many, including those with babes in arms, would rise at six o'clock in all kinds of weather to be at the front of the queue when the shops opened at nine. The fortunate ones would get a bit of bacon, or cheese, or brown sugar, a lump of mutton fat or, sometimes, horse-flesh. But many were turned away disappointed, when the door was closed and a notice put in the window: 'SORRY, SOLD OUT', or 'TRY AGAIN TOMORROW'. In some shops it was 'CLOSED FOR THE DURATION'. Hoarding food was considered a great crime. Lots of poor people in our district were fined for hoarding. No sympathy was shown for the fact that many of these people had several young mouths to feed. But often I would hear my dad say, 'It's one law for the rich and one for the poor.' It was always the rich that got away with everything in those days.

Winnie was lifting the curtain every few seconds, to see if the boys were coming. Suddenly she dropped the curtain and called out, 'Katie! Come on, hide! Quick! On the stairs. The priest's comin' 'ere.'

'Good evening,' we heard him say as he marched in.

But Mrs Nashe sounded annoyed. 'An' what do you want this time, Father? There's no whiskey, if that's what you've come for.'

'I've called to see your good husband,' he replied.

'Well, you'll have a long journey if you want to see him. He's in France, doin' his bit for his king and country.'

'And when will you be joining up, my good lad?' he asked Willie.

But Willie didn't answer. We heard the door slam behind him.

'He'll go when they're ready to call him up,' was his mother's reply. 'An' it would do some good to the likes of *you*, to take off your dog collars an' put on some khaki an' help them lads that's over there, instead of hidin' under that frock you're wearin'!'

'We cannot all go, some of us have to stay at home,' he replied calmly. 'But what I've really come about is to ask you if you'll come to Mass some time.'

'No!' we heard her reply angrily. 'I've got no time for to hear you breathin' hell fire an' damnation at every poor unfortunate sinner you happen to cast your eyes on.'

'Well, I'll call again. In the meantime, I'll pray for you, and your family. Good evening.'

'You'd do better to pray for them poor buggers out there, who need it,' she called out as he closed the door.

As soon as he'd gone, we came out from our hiding place. Pulling Winnie towards her, Mrs Nashe cried out, 'An' *you*, Winnie, don't you ever let me catch you or know you go in that confession box again!'

'No, Mum,' she replied.

Her mother had just about calmed down, when there came another knock at the door.

'Come in, lads,' she said, as she opened the door. 'The girls are here already, waitin' for you.'

While she was putting the kettle on the fire to boil, Winnie introduced me.

'Katie, this is Joe. Joe, this is Katie. An' this is *my* fellow, 'arry,' she said, putting her hand on his face and stroking it.

I thought Joe looked quite a handsome chap with his dark wavy hair. He was wearing a well-cut dark blue suit, and he sounded so polite, when he spoke, saying 'Very pleased to meet you, Katie.' Foolish me, I thought I had fallen in love for the first time in my life, and started to blush.

At that moment Willie came back in, and the three boys started chatting together.

Winnie said, 'Do yer like 'im?'

'Yes,' I whispered, feeling myself blush again.

'I knew yer would. I've been out with 'em both a couple of times.'

When we sat down to eat Joe was quite the gentleman, pulling out my chair for me to sit next to him. I felt very uncomfortable, as each time I looked up from the table I saw Willie's eyes on me. When he actually winked at me, I felt I could have got up and slapped his face. I was glad when it was time to go.

As I left, Willie whispered, 'See yer later, Kate.'

'Not if I can 'elp it!' I whispered back fiercely.

Winnie's mother called after us, 'Mind you behave your-selves, an' don't forget, I want you back by ten.'

It was now eight o'clock, and we were too late for the pictures. Harry and Winnie decided we should all go for a walk. It was a lovely moonlit night, you could almost read a paper.

'Do yer mind not goin' ter the pictures?' Joe asked.

'No,' I replied, 'I think I'd rather go for a walk.'

Winnie and Harry walked in front, with their arms around each other. And as we followed behind, Joe asked if I'd mind if he put his arm around my waist. I blushed, and said I didn't mind. As I felt him gently pull me closer and squeeze my waist, I got my first thrill. It was a wonderful sensation, one that I'd never experienced before.

We walked on and on. I didn't care where he was leading me. Eventually he stopped, and asked if I'd mind standing in a doorway while he lit his cigarette. As he lit up I asked where Winnie and Harry were.

'They'll see us when they pass by,' he replied.

I stood there, and as soon as he put out his cigarette, he hugged me close to him. 'I'm very fond of yer, Katie,' he said, as he placed both hands on my shoulders. 'Will yer be my regular?'

'Yes, Joe,' I replied. 'But I'll have to go now, it's getting late. I'll see yer termorra.'

But as he didn't answer, I looked up into his face and in the moonlight I saw his eyes staring at me. They were sort of glistening; his mouth too was wide open. He looked so funny, I could almost have laughed. But something inside me told me this was no laughing matter. Then, as he drew me closer, he said, 'Will yer let me kiss yer, Katie, just once?'

Like a silly young girl, I trusted him. But as I put my lips close to his, I felt his mouth all wet and his tongue trying to prise open my teeth. I pushed him away. 'Don't do that, Joe!' I cried out. 'It's dirty, an' I don't like it.'

'But I love yer, Katie. Only this once.'

'No!' I yelled, but as I pushed his hands away from my shoulders, he suddenly grabbed my right breast and squeezed it hard and began to rub himself up and down against me. With his other hand he tried to lift up my skirt. I felt humiliated, afraid, and angry, and with all the strength I could muster I pushed him away from me. While I was straightening my clothes, he asked me to forgive him.

'I'm sorry, please forgive me, I don't know what came over me, please forgive me, Katie,' he kept pleading. 'I promise this won't happen again.'

'Yer won't get the bloody chance!' I replied angrily.

At that moment I had the sudden thought that I might have lost my mother's brooch in the struggle. I put my hand on my breast and found, to my relief, that it was still there. He came closer to me and asked again if he was forgiven. I said 'Yes.' When he told me he wasn't going to touch me again, I dropped my hand down and suddenly I felt a clammy piece of flesh. It was his 'peter', hanging limp. All at once I went berserk. Not knowing what I was doing, I grabbed it with my two hands and gripped it tight, as I tried to pull it away from me.

'Let go! Let go!' I heard him scream.

When I did let go, I saw him double up. As he fell to the ground, I ran away, leaving him there.

I didn't realise the time until I heard the clock in the distance strike eleven. I kept running, thinking he would catch up with me. Several couples I ran past stopped to stare, but I was too scared to speak or tell anyone. When I got to the end of the Sandpits I was panting and I had to slow down to a walk. I had only walked a few yards when I noticed a steaming puddle on the pavement. When I looked up to see where it was coming from I got another fright. Coming out of a doorway was a dirty drunken old tramp, trying to put his peter back inside his trousers. When he saw me, he tried to bar my way. "ello, me luv,' he managed to splutter.

Quickly I pushed him over, and as he fell down into his puddle I started to run again. When I reached our house I found the door was bolted. I flopped down on the step and broke down and wept. I knew what to expect, if I banged on the door. It would be another beating. But I couldn't stay there all night. I was afraid of the tramp too now, in case he knew me, or knew where I lived, and came after me. I thought of staying in the brewhouse till the morning, but that was out of the question. The neighbours would find me if I fell asleep, for some of them always rose at dawn to start their washing. I couldn't sleep in the closet, the stench would be too unbearable. There was only one thing to do. I'd go down our cellar, and hope for the best.

I walked back up the yard, and took off the wet, smelly piece of matting, and prayed the cellar grating was not padlocked. To my relief the rusty grating yielded. Slowly, not to make a noise, I lifted it up and slid down on my bottom, inside, among the rubbish. I stood there for a couple of seconds, but everything seemed quiet and still. Even the rats and cockroaches must have gone to sleep. When I climbed the steps and entered the pantry, I took off my shoes and quietly crept up the stairs. I was relieved when I stopped on the first landing, everything was still quiet. But when I reached the attic I saw my sister Liza sitting up in bed, reading her tuppenny romance book by the light from the candle.

I flopped down on the bed and sobbed.

'Where've yer bin?' she whispered. 'Yer know what time is it?'

I shook my head.

'It's nearly twelve o'clock! Come on, I want ter know where yer bin, an' what yer bin doin'.'

'It's a long story, Liza. I'm frightened, an' tired, let me tell yer all about it termorra,' I managed to say.

'Well, 'ow did yer get in the 'ouse, then? It was bolted.'

'I climbed down the cellar. But why did Mum bolt me out?' I whispered back.

'She dain't know yer was out, I 'ad ter lie fer yer. When she called up the stairs an' shouted if yer was in, I told 'er, yes, yer was fast asleep.'

'Thank yer, Liza, I'll treat yer termorra, or try an' get yer some more Woodbines. Now, move over, I'm tired. *Please.*'

'Not before yer brush them cobwebs out of yer 'air.'

As soon as I gave it a good brush, I undressed and quickly got in bed beside her, and while she began to read again, I tried to get to sleep. But suddenly there was a bang on the outside door. I sprang up in bed, trembling like a leaf.

'Oh, my God! It's 'im!' I cried out.

'I don't know what yer bin up to, but yer betta be quiet. They might go away if nobody answers it.'

But there was still more knocking, louder the second time, as we sat up to listen. Then we heard Mum's bedroom window open.

'Who's that down theea? Knockin' on my dower this time o' mornin'.' she yelled down into the yard.

'It's me.'

'Who's me?'

'Willie.'

'Willie who?'

'Willie Nashe.'

'I wonder what 'e wants, Liza?' I whispered anxiously.

''ush, an' listen,' she replied.

'Is yower Katie in?'

'O' course she's in! Fast asleep! Where yow should be! Any'ow, what yer wanta know fer?'

'Me mother wanted ter know if Katie 'ad seen our Winnie, I've looked everywhere, an' we can't find 'er.'

'Well, she ain't 'ere. Katie's bin in bed since ten o'clock.'

We heard the window slam down, but we also heard Mum's footsteps coming up the stairs.

'Get down the bed quickly, pretend yer asleep.'

Quickly Liza blew out the candle and lay down too, hiding her novel under the pillow. But Mum had already seen the light go out.

'What 'ave I told you about readin' in bed? Next time I see one o' them luv-sick books, I'll put it on the fire!' she yelled, as she lit the candle.

I was now more scared than ever. I thought, any moment now she's going to pull the clothes off me. Then I heard her say, ''ow long did yer say Katie's bin asleep?'

'Since about ten o'clock, Mum. Why?'

'Willie Nashe's bin bangin' on the dower, askin' if she'd seen their Winnie.'

''ow could she? She's bin with me all night.'

'Very well, but she'll be sorry if I ever do see 'er with 'er. That Winnie's too old in the 'ead fer 'er years. Now, blow that candle out, an' remember what I said about novels!'

'Yes, goodnight, Mum,' Liza replied.

But Mum went down the stairs without answering. As soon as I heard her bed creak, I sprang up. 'Thank yow fer lyin' fer me, Liza, but I don't want yer ter get inter trouble, if she finds out.'

'Yow leave that ter me, an' remember, I want an explanation termorra. Now, lie down an' let's get ter sleep.'

'Yes, Liza,' I yawned, for I felt safe now I was in my bed. And as soon as my head touched the pillow, I fell asleep.

My mother always let us sleep a little later on Sunday mornings, and when I awoke I saw Liza was reading her tuppenny paperback book. I quickly glanced at the title: *Mill Girl Marries Her Boss*. When she saw me looking over her shoulder, she cried out 'Yer awake then?' and hid the book. 'Now! Come on, I want yer ter tell me what 'appened last night.'

I had hoped she'd forget to ask. I said it didn't matter now. But she was insistent. While I was telling her, I noticed she kept on smiling.

'What yer smilin' at? I can't see nothin' ter smile about. In fact I'm still scared to go outside now. I thought that knockin' last night was 'im, or the tramp, an' it could 'ave bin the police.'

'No need ter be scared, yer might not see 'im again.'

'But what if 'e's still there? An' e's dead?' I asked.

'Yer can't kill a bloke that way, yer silly. But yer very likely ruptured 'im,' she added.

'What's that mean? Ruptured?' I asked.

'Yer'll find out soon enough when yer older,' she replied.

Suddenly I lost my temper. 'Yer all the same in this bloody 'ouse!' I snapped. 'I'm near enough sixteen, and not one of yer'll tell what I should or shouldn't know about life, or sex.'

'Well, yer liked 'im, dain't yer? Or yer wouldn't 'ave gone with 'im.'

'Er . . . yes, an' I believed 'im when 'e said 'e loved me, an' wanted me ter be 'is regular.'

'What did yer feel like when yer first touched it?'

'I wanted to be sick. It felt like a limp wet sausage. I'll never trust another fellow as long as I live.'

'We all say that, Katie, but nature sometimes plays tricks with our feelin's.'

'Do yer think I should tell me dad, or Frankie, Liza?'

'No!' she snapped. 'Yer betta not! Best if yer try an' forget it.'

As I put on my camisole I felt my breast was sore where Joe had squeezed it. I shuddered, remembering it all again. And for weeks, no matter how many times I washed my hands, I could never wash away the thought, and the feel, of that clammy piece of flesh in my hands.

I stayed indoors all Sunday, and when Mum asked me why, I said I didn't feel well. I didn't go to work on Monday either, for I only felt safe when I was indoors. During the morning I heard the newspaper boy call out 'Special! Special! Read all about it!' I began to tremble with fear. Had they found him, and would the police come to arrest me? I had to buy a paper to read what was special. As the newsboy came towards me I opened the door a little way, handed him a penny and snatched the *Birmingham Daily Mail* from him. I looked down at the 'latest' column and saw the words 'Two German U-Boats Sunk'. Then I scanned the paper all over. I was relieved to find nothing about the incident, but I wasn't satisfied till I had examined another paper, and another. After that I plucked up the courage to go out.

I thought I had better find out why Willie had been enquiring about his sister. Putting my fears to one side, I knocked on the Nashes' door. But when Mrs Nashe appeared, she yelled at me: 'What do you want?'

'Is Winnie in, Mrs Nashe?' I asked timidly.

'Yes, she is! An' it was one o'clock in the mornin' when she came home! An' she's had a beltin'. An' I've locked her in her room till she's ready to tell me where she's been.'

'But it ain't my fault, Mrs Nashe,' I replied. 'We were goin' ter stay together, but Winnie an' 'er fellow wandered off on their own.'

'I don't want to hear any more excuses. So you'd better not call again. An' she's not goin' with any more fellows, either, until I get the truth out of her. Now bugger off! And she slammed the door in my face.

I couldn't understand why Mrs Nashe had to blame me. It wasn't my fault Winnie had come home at one o'clock in the morning. As I walked back home I kept wondering where Winnie had been that night.

Two days later, as I was walking down Narstone Lane, someone tapped me on my shoulder. When I turned around and saw Joe standing there, I cried out, 'What yer want now?'

'I've been lookin' fer yer, Katie, each morning, to tell yer 'ow sorry I am,' he replied, as he put his two hands on my shoulders.'

'Too late fer that now! An' take yer 'ands off my shoulders!' I snapped.

As I went to walk away, he said, 'Don't go yet, Katie, *please*. I want yer to hear what I've got ter say, then yer can go.'

He looked so sad that I couldn't help but say, 'Very well, but I can only spare you a few minutes.'

'I really do love yer, Katie, please believe me, and I'm sorry for what 'appened on Saturday night.'

'I'm sorry too,' I replied, 'but now I must go.'

As I went to move away, he said would I see him again, and he would prove how sorry he was.

'Why?' I asked.

'I've had my calling up papers, an' I leave in two days' time. I'd like to see yer again before I go.'

'Very well. Where?'

'Can I see yer at eight o'clock tomorrow night, by Chamberlain clock?'

'Very well,' I answered.

As I walked away, I looked back. Seeing him still standing there looking all forlorn, I began to feel sorry for him. After all he'd tried to do to me, I still liked him. Suddenly, on impulse I ran back and kissed his cheek. Neither of us spoke, but when I hurried down the street again, I looked back, and saw him wave. I waved back. During that afternoon, while I was working, I kept thinking about him, wondering whether I should meet him or not. I asked myself, had I been foolish to promise to meet him? Was this a trick to punish me for what I did to him? I thought I'd ask Liza to advise me what I should do. When we sat up in bed that night, I told her all about it.

She yelled at me, 'After all 'e tried ter do ter yer? Yer want ter see 'im again? If yer tek my advice, Katie, yer'll keep away from 'im. In my opinion 'e sounds very plausible.'

'I don't think so, Liza, 'e's really nice when yer get ter know 'im.'

'Yer've only bin out with 'im once! Yer can't tell me yer know 'is ways by that! Do yer still like 'im?' she asked.

'Yes, Liza, but I don't know why. I feel I want ter see 'im an' yet I don't. I really don't know what ter do.'

'On second thoughts, would yer like me ter go an' see 'im?' she asked.

'Yes, Liza, an' tell him 'ow sorry I am, but I'm not too well.'

'Leave it to me, I'll find some excuse. I want ter see what 'e's like, any'ow.'

Next day I took the long way round to work and back, in case I should bump into him. So I was late getting home. When I walked in, I was surprised to see that Mum and Dad were dressed in their Sunday best.

'Where yer bin till now?' Mum snapped at once.

'I felt like some fresh air an' took the long way 'ome,' I replied.

'Very well,' my dad said, 'come an' get yer tea, luv. I want ter tek yer mum out, it's 'er birthday.'

Usually birthdays in our house just came and went. Our family were not ones to show any outward love or affection. Though sometimes my dad would tap my head, or stroke my hair, when I said goodnight.

Mum and Dad left, and my brother followed soon after to go courting his girl, Nellie. Then I watched as Liza put on her 'war paint' and her best hat, coat and gloves. I really didn't feel well now, I was so nervous, wondering if I'd done the right thing.

'Wake me up if I'm asleep when yer come in, Liza, an' tell me what 'e says.'

'Okay,' she replied, as she closed the door behind her.

Ten o'clock came, and Liza hadn't returned. I lay in bed, imagining all kinds of things that might have happened. I seemed to have been lying there for hours before I heard her climb the stairs.

'Where yer bin till now?' I cried out as I sat up in bed. 'I've bin worryin' meself sick about yer.'

'Yer know where I went!' she snapped.

'But it didn't afta tek yer all this time!' I replied angrily.

'I 'ad ter go ter see me own young man, didn't I? An' it was late. We 'ad a few words, 'e was going to leave me, but when I told 'im why I was late, we made up.'

'I'm sorry,' I said. 'I forgot you had to meet George. Are you both all right now?' I added.

'Yes. But, Katie, yer should really 'ave gone yerself to see 'im, 'e was really disappointed, when yer didn't come yerself.'

'What did yer say?' I asked eagerly.

'I made the excuse yer was poorly in bed. An' yer know what? 'e's a real nice, 'onest bloke.'

'Maybe 'e is, Liza, but there was no reason why 'e should try to molest me that night.'

'Katie,' she replied, 'they all try it once, an' if yer give way, yer never see 'em again. But if yer refuse, they really respect yer, that's why 'e wanted ter see yer again. Yer understand what I mean?'

'Yes, Liza, an' thank yer fer goin'. But perhaps I should 'ave gone ter meet 'im, Liza.'

'It's too late now, 'e catches the early morning train for France termorra. But I gave 'im our address an' 'e said 'e'd write ter yer, an' would yer wait fer 'im when 'e comes back 'ome again. The way 'e spoke, Katie, I believe 'e really, truly loves yer,' she added.

Tears began to flow now as I said, 'Yes, Liza. If 'e writes, I'll tell 'im I'll wait fer 'im.'

'Now, there's no need fer tears, by the time 'e comes back from the war yer'll be able ter mek yer mind up. Now let's both get ter sleep.'

But all through the night, off and on, I kept thinking about him, and for many more nights too. A couple of months later I received a beautiful lace-edged card from him. On the top right-hand corner was a picture of a young soldier, gazing down to a girl in the left-hand corner. Printed in gilt letters were the words 'You are always in my thoughts, my darling.' On the back of the card there were a few lines to say he would always think of me and when the war was over he would come to see me again. He ended, 'God bless you, Katie, all my love, Joe, xxxx.'

I treasured that card for years. But, sad to say, I never saw or heard from Joe again. I couldn't even write, for I had no forwarding address. I didn't even know his surname, or where he lived.

6

Winnie's Trouble

After the Saturday night we made up that foursome, I didn't see
Winnie for weeks. Then I saw her in the fish and chip shop.
She was muffled up in a scarf, but, when she turned around, I
noticed that her face was swollen and bruised. She hurried past
me, but I caught up with her.

'What yer done ter yer face, Winnie?' I asked, 'An' why yer
bin avoidin' me?'

Suddenly, she began to weep. When I asked her what was
wrong, she said, 'I can't tell yer now, I've got ter 'urry back
'ome.'

'Well, why is yer face all bruised?' I asked.

She drew the scarf closer around her face and wept.

When I asked her why she was crying, she said, 'I can't tell
yow 'ere, but can I come to your 'ouse an' see yer, when yer
mum's out, then I'll tell yer all about it?'

'Yes, Winnie,' I replied eagerly. 'I shall be by myself Saturday
night, will that do?'

'Yes, I'll try,' she managed to say, through her tears.

'Say about eight o'clock, then you can tell me all about it,
now don't cry any more, tek my 'anky.'

As she wiped away the tears, she said, 'I'll 'ave ter go now,
before Mum misses me.'

For the next few days, until Saturday evening, I worried
about her. Had she fallen down somewhere? Or had she been
beaten? Or was it something more serious?

Eight o'clock. I waited. Half past eight. A quarter to nine. I had almost given up hope when she knocked on the door. 'Come on in, Winnie,' I cried out. 'The door's open.'

When she came in, I saw that her eyes were still red from weeping.

'Come an' sit down Winnie, by the fire, while I mek yer a nice 'ot cuppa tea.'

As we sat facing each other, drinking our tea, I asked, 'Why 'aven't yer bin ter see me before? It's been nearly two months now.'

'Mum won't let me out of 'er sight since that Saturday night,' she replied at once.

'Then 'ow yer come ter get out now?'

'She's gone ter see me aunt. But I can't stop long. I afta get back before she misses me.'

'She blames yow, Katie, fer keepin' me out that night.'

'But it wasn't my fault!' I cried, indignantly. 'Yow left me and Joe, and walked off on yer own! An' if it 'adn't been fer my sister sayin' I was in bed early I should 'ave bin in trouble too.'

'I told 'er it wasn't your fault, I told 'er we got lost. But she still didn't believe me.'

'Where did yer get to, then?' I asked, as I saw the tears run down her face again.

'I 'aven't told anyone. But I think I can trust you, Katie.'

I tried to comfort her by saying I'd always liked her no matter what she'd said or done, and as I wiped away her tears, she began to tell me.

''arry asked me ter go to 'is 'ome ter meet 'is dad, but when we got there, 'e was out. We sat on the sofa, an' while we waited, we kept drinkin' port. I don't know 'ow many glasses I had, but I was feeling drowsy. But I remember 'arry sayin' 'ow much 'e loved me, would I marry 'im when the war was over. Then, after we snuggled close together, we kissed, and made love. A little while after I began to feel ashamed fer givin' in to 'im. But 'e said again 'e loved me, and 'e'd save up an' we could be married an' would I wait ter see 'is father. But I wanted ter get 'ome. I 'ad no idea of the time. So I asked 'im ter see me 'ome. On the way 'e kissed me again an' we promised ter see each other next day. But when I got indoors, Mum was waitin' fer me, with the leather strap.'

'But I always thought your mum was a kind, gentle woman?' I said, surprised.

'A lot of people think that, but yer don't know my mum, she belted me, an' locked me in the attic, an' I 'ad ter stay there till she was ready ter let me out. A few weeks later I kept feelin' sick an' when she knew I couldn't eat my food she almost dragged me ter the doctor's. He examined me, an' told Mum I was in the family way. On the way back 'ome she kept callin' me bad names, an' when we got indoors she beat me again. Then she locked me in a second time, an' went to see my aunt, ter see what could be done about me. Then, ter make matters worse, a telegram came from the War Office ter say my dad was missin'. And when Mum read it, she flopped down in the chair an' began to cry. I felt shocked too when I read it, but when I went ter put my arms round 'er, ter try ter console 'er, she punched me in the face an' called me a dirty little slut. She was still 'ittin' me, when me aunt walked in. She screamed at Mum. I 'eard 'er say, "Yer can't knock it out of 'er that way." An' she said she knew of a woman who could give me an abortion. But Mum screamed back at 'er and said I was goin' into the work'ouse or the home fer fallen women. I'm scared now, Katie. I don't know what ter do.'

Tears filled my eyes too as I said, 'Why don't yer go an' see 'arry an' tell 'im? If 'e said 'e loves yer, surely 'e'll marry yer?'

'But that's the worst of it, Katie, 'e don't know. When I went to see 'im, 'is father said 'e'd joined the Navy, and when I told 'is dad I was goin' ter 'ave 'is baby, 'e said 'e didn't believe me, an' I was to find some other silly bugger ter put the blame on. I don't know what ter do now, Katie, Mum's took all my clothes away, an' I've got no money. I'd run away, but there's nowhere to go to, only my aunt's, and I'm even scared of 'er now.'

'I only wish I could 'elp yer, Winnie. Pr'aps in a few days when yer mum's got over 'er grief, she'll change 'er mind. But in the meantime if yer'll come an' see me termorra night I can let yer 'ave four pounds from my post office savings.'

'But I don't know when I shall be able to pay you back, or when I can get out ter see yer again.'

'You will,' I said, as I wiped away her tears. 'Yer'll find out

later, when yer near yer time, she'll be sorry fer beatin' yer an'
callin' yer names.'

'I'll pray each night an' hope yer right, Katie. I must go now,
before she comes 'ome. An' thank yer fer listenin' ter me. I feel a
bit better now I've told yer about it. But promise yer'll not say I've
bin 'ere, or say anythin' about my condition to anyone.'

'Yer can trust me, Winnie,' I managed to say as I kissed her
wet, swollen face.

As I watched her go down the street I went indoors and cried,
and prayed to the Good Lord to forgive her mother, and to bring
them closer together. And I thought how lucky I was. The same
thing could have happened to me, that night.

I waited for Winnie the next night and for several nights, but
she never came. The following Sunday I plucked up courage to go
to her mum's house but when I got there I found the house
empty. All the furniture had gone, and there was a notice stuck
inside the window: 'THIS HOUSE TO LET. KEY AT NUMBER SIX,
RENT 7/6 per week.'

When I called at number six the woman said she didn't know
much about them. She didn't even know they'd left, until the
landlord gave her the key to let the house to the next tenant. It
was several years before I saw Winnie again. But each night I
would mention her in my prayers, and ask the Good Lord to
watch over her in her hour of need.

7

Improving Myself

I'm afraid my romantic feelings for Joe didn't stop me being attracted to other young fellows. And Liza was right, the memory of my struggle with him didn't really make me wary.

One day the forewoman where I worked asked me to help sort out some files in the office. Writing at the desk was a young man so handsome I couldn't take my eyes off him. As soon as the forewoman left the room, I said, 'Yer new 'ere, ain't yer?'

'Beg pardon?' he replied pleasantly.

'I said, yer new 'ere?'

'Yes,' he replied, smiling.

I could see he wanted to say more, but when the forewoman entered he went back to his writing.

'That'll be all,' she said. 'Thank you for helping me out.'

'Oh, that's all right, I'll be glad to any time.'

As I went through the glass door, I looked back and saw him smile at me.

I saw him several times during the next two weeks, when he came through the workshop. Then one afternoon he came up to the bench where I was working.

'Excuse my asking, but I was wondering if you'd come for a walk with me on Saturday afternoon?'

All the girls' eyes were watching us, but I didn't care. In fact, I felt highly honoured. I agreed to meet him outside the corner tea shop in Victoria Street at two o'clock. As soon as the eagerly awaited afternoon came, I dressed in my best and put on a bit of 'war paint', then I had only to slip a perfumed

'Phul-nana' card down between my breasts, and I was ready to go.

As soon as he saw me coming around the corner, he came towards me, and as he raised his hat I thought he was the handsomest fellow I'd ever been out with.

'I'm glad you were able to come,' he said.

'Oh, I always keep me promise.'

We went inside and he ordered tea and cream cakes, and while we sat eating he told me his name was Richard Evans and he lived in Monument Road. (Oh dear, I thought, among the posh nobs.)

'My name's Kathleen,' I said.

But he said he already knew, from the clocking-in cards. I was glad he didn't ask where I lived.

After we had our tea he asked if I'd like to take a walk with him around St Paul's Church. He was so polite, not saucy like other fellows I'd met. After that we walked out together every Saturday afternoon for several weeks.

One lovely warm afternoon we walked along by Wasson Pool. I began to smile as I thought of the last time when I was here with Winnie, when I'd seen my dad and Winnie's dad rising up out of the canal naked, carrying coal above their heads. When he asked me why I was smiling I told him it was a long story, but maybe I'd tell him some time.

'Shall we sit down by this tree?' he asked, taking off his coat for me to sit on.

We sat there talking for a few minutes. Then he asked me if he could kiss me. I just nodded. But as soon as he had kissed me, he said, 'I think we had better be moving, Kathleen, it's getting late.'

'Yes,' I replied, as I handed him his coat. 'I've gorra go too, or I'll get in trouble with me mum.'

'Kathleen, I like you a lot, you're a very nice girl and very attractive but . . .'

'But what?' I asked.

'I hope you won't be offended, but I'd like you better if you didn't put that rubbish on your face.'

I lost my temper at once. 'If yer don't like me as I am yer know what yer can do!' I snapped, as I went to walk away.

'Don't go. I'm sorry if I offended you. I wanted really to help you. I could help you speak nicely and properly.'

'What yer mean, speak properly?'

'Not to say "gorra" when you really mean "got to", or "have to", and several other words you say. If you spoke correctly you'd go a long way, Kathleen, believe me,' he replied, as he took my hand.

'But I can't 'elp 'ow I speak!' I snapped.

'But you can, if you'll let me teach you.'

'It's all right for yow, p'raps yow've 'ad an education, but I ain't. My teacher did 'er best for me, when I was a young girl. I was gettin' along fine well, until I tried practisin' at 'ome, then when I tried talkin' as I'd been told ter my mum, she said "Don't come 'ere talkin' like that with yer bloody airs an' graces!" An' then I gave up. Yer see, Richard, it's 'ard when yer don't know any different, an' yer 'ear it all around yer, day in an' day out.'

'I understand. Next time we meet, I'll bring you a book and you can practise with me.'

'I'm not stupid, yer know!' I said, flaring up once more. 'I can read, an' write, an' add up, an' subtract!'

'But that's not everything. You see, I like you a lot, and I'd like to take you to meet my parents, but . . .'

'But what?' I cried out angrily.

'Until you let me teach you to speak correctly, I don't think they would approve, and you'd feel hurt.'

At that I really lost my temper. 'Well, if it's yer parents yer worried about, I won't bother ter see yer any more.'

As I walked quickly away, he came after me, but when he asked me again to try, I felt very hurt and angry. I slapped his face, and ran. When I went to work on the Monday morning I did my best to avoid him. He tried to speak to me several times, but I always turned away. And when I heard some of the girls say we'd had a lovers' tiff, and make some other remarks as well, I left that job to work at another firm.

I never saw Richard Evans again, but I often remembered what he had tried to tell me. As it happened, I found that the girls and women at my new firm were very kind and spoke very politely. I

knew now that I wanted to speak correctly, and I tried to learn by
listening to them, and copying the way they spoke.

I tried practising when I was at home, but it wasn't easy. My
sister sneered, and my mother ranted. 'Yer bloody fool,' she'd
shout. 'Yer know where that bloody talk'll get yer! On the road
ter ruin, that's what!'

But I ignored them both. I was determined to learn to speak
correctly, and I kept up my efforts. Sometimes I'd hide in the
brewhouse, or the yard lav, to practise. But I was too ignorant in
those days even to know there was such a thing as a dictionary. It
was only by listening to others that I was able to educate myself
enough to adapt and get by.

8

The End of the War

One very cold, dark night, while Dad, Liza, Frankie and me were sitting at the table waiting for Mum to dish out our supper, we saw our brother Jack stagger inside the door, with his laden kit bag. As he flung it on the floor, we all rushed to welcome him home.

Mum threw her arms around him, saying, 'When do yer go back?'

Jack began to laugh. 'I've only just got 'ere, Mum.'

'Yer know what 'er meant ter say, son,' said Dad. 'Any'ow, 'ow long are yer 'ere for?'

'I've only got seven days furlough, Dad, I go back Sunday night. I've been travellin' all day, it was a slow train, and we were packed like sardines, sailors and soldiers. Lots o' poor, tired bleeders 'ad ter stand in the guard's van, an' in cattle trucks. I'm glad ter be 'ome, Ma, I'm tired, an' I'm clammed.

While Mum dished up some supper for Jack, Dad slipped out to get him a drink. When he came back, with a half-gallon stone jar of ale, he said. 'We're goin' ter celebrate when yer've 'ad yer supper, son, an' 'ave a few neighbours in.'

But Jack had other priorities. 'Not ternight, Dad. I'd like a bath, I'm lousy. Is there any place I could go?'

'I'm sorry, son, the public baths are closed ternight. But after you've 'ad summat to eat, I'll light a fire under the copper in the brew'ouse.'

Then Dad said Grace, and thanked the Lord for sending Jack home safely.

After we had eaten, we all set to, fetching and carrying water from the tap in the yard, to fill the boiler. When the water had heated up we had to ladle it out into the maiding tub, for Jack to stand in. Dad lit a couple of candles, hung an old blanket over the rusty iron window frame, to keep out the cold, then told us to stand guard outside in case any nosy neighbours or kids came near. But not a soul was to be seen, only us. It was even too cold for our moggy to go courting.

Mum handed Frankie a bottle of Lysol disinfectant and told him to slip it under the blanket. 'An' tell 'im not ter use it all. 'e'll find a piece of carbolic soap be'ind the mangle,' she added.

Next day was Sunday, which was supposed to be a day of rest. But when I heard my mum get up early, unfortunately I got up too and so I had the job of swilling out the brewhouse and filling the copper boiler ready for the Monday morning wash. After I'd finished, and come indoors, I watched my mum turn my brother's khaki tunic and trousers inside out and iron all the seams, to kill the lice and eggs. Next day she washed his shirt, long pants, vest and socks in Lysol.

Although Jack and my parents very seldom saw eye to eye, and they quarrelled frequently before he went in the Army, now Mum and Dad were proud to show him off in the pubs, in front of the neighbours. Mum didn't like it when Jack went to visit the widow he'd ben courting, though. And when he stayed two days and nights of his leave with her, Mum quarrelled with him. Dad said it was his own business and that he was old enough to make his own mind up what to do or where to go. When Mum began weeping he said, 'Let 'im enjoy what short time 'e's got. The Lord only knows when we shall see 'im again, Polly, so let's do the best we can, an' mek 'im 'appy befower 'e goes back ter France.'

Jack's last couple of nights our neighbours were invited to come in, to have a few drinks and sing songs. Jack brought his young woman in too, and while Dad and Jack were giving her plenty of attention, I could see by Mum's face she didn't like her. But there was nothing she could say or do, for Dad had already warned her.

Sunday came all too soon. We all went to see Jack off at the station. The platform was crowded with hundreds of men in different uniforms with kit bags slung over their shoulders, and women and children were crying as they hugged and clung to their loved ones before being parted from them.

The rejoicing when the war ended was in contrast to this scene. There was dancing in the streets, the pubs flung open their doors to distribute free beer, and people gave away food that they had hoarded for years.

My mum, and the neighbours too, forgot all their grievances when she carried out our old gramophone, and we danced up and down the yard, with our skirts held well above our knees, singing:

Knees up Mother Brown,
Yer drawers are comin' down
Get a pin an' pin 'em up,
Before they come right down.

But through it all there were still many thousands grieving for the loved ones they knew would never come back. And when the fighting men were demobilised, bitterness and anger began to grow. The soldiers remembered those promises from politicians, that this war would be the war to end all wars, and England would be a place fit for heroes to live in. They hadn't long returned from the trenches, many with limbs missing, or worse, before they realised that there was only unemployment awaiting them. Nothing but war, it seemed, could provide employment for starving people, and now the war was over the people were starving again.

Those soldiers returned from the 1914–18 war would have been still more bitter if they had realised that the next generation, their sons and daughters, would also be gun fodder for war-mongering politicians.

9

Marriage and Children

On Christmas Eve 1919 I met and began to fall in love with Charlie, who was to be my husband. We were married in 1921. *
Charlie happened to be one of the lucky ones who found employment after he was demobilised, but it was to be for only a short period. I too had work in a factory. Many firms employed women in preference to men: they would do the same work for less wages.

When we were first married we lived in a furnished room. But when my first son was only a couple of months old, and I was already pregnant with my second baby, the landlady gave us notice. I was still working, but Charlie was by then on short time (he was soon to be out of work altogether), and we were very hard up.

I tramped the district far and wide in search of a place to live, but everywhere I met with the same answer, 'No children allowed'. I humbled myself to visit the parish relief offices, but when I asked them if they could find us a place to live, their answer was 'We do not find accommodation for anyone.' Then they added, 'If you have nowhere to live, there is always the workhouse.'

As soon as I got back to the furnished room I broke down and wept. When Charlie came home late that night with the useful coppers he earned by selling sawdust, and I told him what those inquisitors had said, he went wild. 'The workhouse? They told yer the workhouse? After fightin' for a better life an' a place to

* The story of these years is told in *Where There's Life*.

live? They talk about the bleedin' workhouse. If I'd got me rifle here, I'd shoot the bleedin' bastards, and them in the bleedin' Government!'

By now we were really desperate, and though the last place I wanted to live was with my mother, when Mum and Dad said we could move in with them, to live in the attic I had slept in as a child, I had to agree. I promised myself that we would leave as soon as things got better.

Charlie and my dad whitewashed the attic walls, and when they had left to go for a drink in the George and Dragon, I laid my son down on the sofa and set to and scrubbed those worn, knotted boards. All that evening I longed for my mother to come up and help me, or talk to me, but she never came. I broke down and wept.

Until we could get some kind of furniture to put in the attic, my husband, my baby and myself had to sleep on a mattress on the floor in Mum and Dad's room. Later we were able to buy a second-hand double bed, two ladder-backed chairs, a well-worn kitchen table, and a large wardrobe with an oval front mirror. Later still we bought a couple of grey army blankets from the Army and Navy stores. And some of the neighbours who lived in our yard were very kind and helpful. Although they didn't have much to spare themselves, they gave me a few odd crocks, and lent me some of their utensils until we could afford to buy our own.

When my mother realised that the neighbours were helping to give us a start, she unbent a little. 'Yer can fetch a bit of coal up from down the cellar an' light yerself a fire in the attic grate,' I remember her saying. But I'd to pay for it. In more ways than one.

And so we had to live and sleep in that small attic from the end of 1921 onwards. It was 1931 before I left. And I will remember until the day I die the bitterness of those ten years.

In my ignorance, during this time I gave birth to five children, and had two miscarriages. My eldest son was only six years old when he was knocked down and killed on the way home from school. In that same year, 1927, my dad, whom I loved and was always proud of, died in the workhouse. Soon after, my mother turned to drink, which made our lives more unbearable. Often when she went away for long weekends I'd pray she would never return, but my prayers were not answered.

On 25 April 1931, our tenth wedding anniversary, my husband died. I was told I wasn't entitled to a widow's pension because he hadn't enough insurance stamps. I could only get parish relief, which was not enough for our needs. You weren't allowed to have any earnings while you were on parish relief, but I had to stretch it somehow, and so, after putting my children to bed, I would go out at night selling firewood from door to door. Then someone made it their business to tell the officer in charge of parish relief that I was selling firewood. I had to appear in front of a tribunal, where I was refused any further help, and warned that I would be prosecuted for not declaring my earnings. My children and I were now almost starving. Some of our kind neighbours offered their help with food they themselves could hardly spare, but I couldn't take it.

In total desperation I made a heartbreaking decision: I resolved to let my children go into a home where they would be fed and well cared for, until such time as I could provide a proper home for them, and give them the love and affection they needed. I went to see the matron of Dr Barnardo's home in Moseley, and asked if I could leave the children in their care for a short time, explaining that as soon as I got everything arranged for a better future I would have my children back with me again. I thought this would be a matter of a few weeks. And so it was arranged. But later I found I had made a terrible mistake, in not having it all in writing.

It was a bitterly cold day when I took my children to Moseley Village Home, and left them there in the charge of the matron. I hugged and kissed them and after giving them a few sweets I'd saved I walked away before they saw my tears. I don't remember anything about walking back alone to my mother's house that day. I only remember that when I climbed those dark, narrow attic stairs, and entered that room with so many memories, I broke down completely.

I must have seemed a stranger to them. They had been so young when I parted with them. And though in the intervening years I had sometimes been able to see Kathleen in the home, Jean and Mary had been fostered out, and we had had hardly any contact.

As I began to explain who I was, two elderly women came up to me and one asked if I was Mrs Flood. I replied that I was, and asked her about my son, John. She said her instructions were only to deliver my daughters safely. But before she boarded the train again she wrote down the address of Watts Naval Training School, and said I should enquire about him there.

That night, after tucking the girls up in their beds, I wrote a letter to Watts, asking why my son hadn't been returned to me. A few days later I received a reply saying that my son was now serving on one of His Majesty's ships. After that I wrote several letters explaining that he was only fifteen years old, but I had no more replies. I also wrote to the War Office, but I had no reply from them either. John went all through the war in the Navy.

I did my utmost to make my three daughters happy, trying to make up for the lost years. Kathleen, who was now fourteen, settled in well. Soon she came to help me in my enamelling business. But Jean and Mary, who were twelve and nine, couldn't seem to settle at all. This was not surprising, in the circumstances, but at times it was very hard. I had scarcely got to know Mary when she wanted to be evacuated with the other children from her school. Although I was upset to part with her again so soon, it seemed best to let her do as she wished. I could only pray that the Good Lord would keep her safe and reunite us as soon as the war ended. Meanwhile, as often as we could, we visited her in Wales, where she seemed happy to be with her schoolfriends. Jean, too, was very restless for the first couple of years after she clame back to me. Then, at Kathleen's suggestion, I took her to work in the business as well. She enjoyed that, and began to relax.

Not long after the girls were returned to me, I left the rented house in Albert Road and bought a house in Waverhill Road, off the Soho Road, Handsworth. Only a couple of weeks after we moved, we heard that the house in Albert Road had been bombed. It was then that I realised that this was not only a war for the men in the forces, it was to be a war for the whole population of innocent men, women and little children. Later we were issued with identity cards, gas masks, ration books for food, and coupons for clothing.

Each night, as soon as Radio Luxemburg went off the air, Kathleen and Jean and I would put on our siren suits, so that we were ready to go down the air raid shelter when the warning sirens went. Our shelter was one of several underground store-rooms under some little shops on the corner of our road. They were long nights in the shelters, and none of us knew whether we would be alive to see the dawn. But we had some good times. We did a lot of community singing, to the accompaniment of an accordion and a banjo, and as well we were all expected to do 'turns' to help keep our spirits up.

There was one wonderful character, who was a great contributor to the entertainment. Everyone called her 'Old Molly'. She was a small, round figure of a woman, who always wore a faded red scarf tied over her curlers, an old long brown frock, and a pair of men's boots which had seen better days. She had the job of cleaning out the public lavatories across the road, and you would often see her coming out of the pub opposite, carrying her mop and bucket, with a Guinness or a bottle of Mackeson's stout inside the bucket. When the raids were very bad she'd come down the shelter with her mop and bucket and its contents, ready to go across the street when the all-clear sounded. She would always give us a song, and we would encourage her by throwing pennies in her bucket. But she was artful enough to entertain us with only one chorus each night, knowing she'd be able to collect more coppers in the bucket when she sang to us the next night.

I would sing or tell stories. I remember one night, while there was a lull, I told them some stories about things that had happened when I was a girl: how my family and my granny and an assortment of neighbours went into the country, hop-picking, and how my brother came to steal a pig, and how my mum won her black eye. *

* These stories are told in *Her People*.

While I was talking there was suddenly a screaming whistle outside and a nerve-racking clatter in the street above. All at once Molly yelled out, 'Them bleedin' 'cendiaries! If I 'ad that bleedin' 'itler 'ere, I'd ram this mop down 'is bleedin' throat!'

'Now, now, Molly,' Mrs Fray, one of my neighbours, said quietly. 'There's no use upsettin' everybody, yer must try an' calm yerself down, like the rest of us.'

'But I've gotta go out an' clean the urinals,' she cried out.

'Yer not goin' anywhere,' Mrs Fray replied, 'until them fire bombs 'ave finished droppin'.'

'They won't 'it me! I can put me bucket over me 'ead!'

'You'll stay where yow are!' Mrs Fray replied. 'Any'ow, there'll be enough water in them closets ter clean all of 'em at once themselves, if they do get 'it. Now sit yerself down, Molly, an' keep quiet, an' wait.'

After a lot of coaxing Molly took the bottle of stout from out of the bucket and drank it down, then toppled down on a bunker, making sure she held on to the mop and bucket, before she dozed off. Later, one of the wardens brought several large packets of chips and handed them around while Mrs Fray and I made tea for everyone. Although it went a bit quiet outside, we could still hear the thuds from the bombs in the distance and the fire engines racing down the street. Now and then we could hear one of our big guns (we called it 'Big Emma') firing at the bombers as they roared overhead. While we waited for the all clear, four men came into the shelter. I recognised two of them, our neighbours Mr Turner, the train conductor, and Mr Ellis, who worked at the Co-op; their wives and children had been evacuated. The four of them were covered from head to foot in debris. They told us they'd been in the thick of it, helping the wardens and firemen to put out the incendiaries.

After they had drunk their tea and lit their fags they squatted around an upturned crate and began to play cards. As soon as they heard a warden come in they snatched up the money and spread the crate with matches. But it was too late. He had already seen the money changing hands.

'I ain't 'avin' any gamblin' down 'ere!' he cried out as he came towards them.

'We're only playin' fer matches,' Mr Turner replied.

'Yer don't fool me!' the warden said. 'Yer'd do better if yer'd go outside an' see what yer can do ter help others.'

'Why, yer bloody old sod!' Mr Turner cried out. 'We've bin out theea all night, 'elpin' ter do your job.'

'Ah, an' we don't get paid fer it!' replied Mr Ellis, 'so sod off an' let us alone.'

But by now, the warden had lost his temper.

'Well, if that's yer attitude, if yer don't put them cards away I'll fetch a copper in, ter do it for yer.'

'Yer can fetch the 'ole bloody force in!' Mr Turner replied.

As he went out they began to play again, still playing with matches – but I heard one of them say quietly, 'One match equals a penny. We'll settle up later.' They hadn't been playing long when a policeman entered, followed by the warden.

'Now,' he asked as he walked towards the players, 'what's this I hear about you four gambling?'

'We're not gamblin', Constable,' Mr Ellis remarked. 'As yer can see, we're only playin' with matches.'

'Oh well, carry on lads, as long as you don't cause any trouble, there's nothing I can do.'

As soon as the officer left, the warden became fuming, and went out and brought in another policeman, who was not so easy-going. He didn't believe them, and he tipped the crate over and told them to clear off out. There was such a skirmish, the policeman's hat fell off.

'Leave 'em alone, they ain't been doin' any 'arm,' Mrs Fray piped up. 'Pity yow ain't got better things to do.'

'You keep out of this, missus,' he replied.

'She's speaking the truth,' I replied. 'We all saw them playing with matches.'

The Constable left the shelter, but as soon as he got up the steps outside we heard him blow his whistle. Another policeman arrived, and the gamblers were arrested and taken to the police station. Next morning they were carted off in the Black Maria to the law courts, where they were tried. Mrs Fray and I and several other women, including Old Molly with her mop and bucket, went to give evidence. But there was no need really for us to have gone; the magistrate just cautioned them and said they were to behave in future. After that night the warden was known around as 'Mr Nark'.

I often felt sorry for Old Molly and so did everyone else who knew her. But she was always very independent-minded.

One night I said, 'Molly, there's a widow who lives a few doors from me, she wants a cleaner, she'll pay you well, better than that stinking, messy job you're doing.'

'I'll thank yer ter mind yer own business!' she snapped. 'I like doin' me job. It's me life.'

I did my best to talk her round, but in the end I gave up. Then one night we missed her coming down the shelter to sing and do a knees-up. Later we were told she had been killed while on her rounds.

11

Mary and Mum

One cold day in February 1941, I happened to be standing in the queue outside the greengrocer's in Icknield Street. It was my birthday, and I was trying to buy some extra fruit to give my daughters a treat when they came home from work. I felt someone tap me on the shoulder, and turning around I was very surprised to see my eldest sister, Mary. We threw our arms around each other.

'I'm so happy to see you, Kate,' she cried out tearfully.

'Me too, Mary,' I managed to say as we hugged and kissed each other.

'How long has it been since I saw you last, Kate?'

'The last time was over three years ago. You were making doughnuts, and you threw the tray at Bill's old horse for eating 'em. Remember?'*

We both began to laugh, and she added, 'Yes, and it was a pity they didn't put him in the knacker's yard with the old mare.'

'How are you getting on with him now?' I asked.

'Oh, it's a long story. Maybe I'll tell you all about it some day,' she replied. 'Anyhow, when you've got what you've come for, let's go over the road and have a drink. You don't know how glad I am to see you again, Kate,' she added.

I was very surprised, the way she kept chattering, for I'd always remembered her as a very quiet person, who kept herself within herself.

We went into the pub, and she had a gin and I had my favourite

* The story of these years is told in *Where There's Life*.

Mackeson's stout. While we sat drinking and chatting I happened to notice Mary's husband over in the bar.

'Bill's in there,' I pointed out.

'And he can stay there for all I care,' she replied bitterly.

'Are you two at loggerheads still?' I asked.

'We have been since we came back from America.'

'Why? Didn't you like it?'

'I did, and I made lots of friends, but he was such a bighead and so sarcastic to the people I met, they didn't get along with him. I kept making excuses for him, but it wasn't easy to convince them.'

When we left the pub, she asked if I had time to come over home with her. I said I would but couldn't stay long. She had a beautiful home. Everything was spick and span. I stayed long enough to have a cup of tea, then promised I'd call again.

She said, 'Will you try and come next Saturday? Bill's going to Slough to see his mother and sister for the weekend, and I'll be by myself. There's such a lot I want to tell you, and I may never get another chance.'

On the following Saturday afternoon I kept my promise and went to see Mary. As we sat drinking our tea, she told me that she had saved enough money to buy a small lock-up shop.

'I'm selling ladies' and children's dresses and underwear, and other kinds of odds and ends. But I'll be doing better still when the coupons come off the clothes. You'll have to come and have a look at it some time, and see if there's anything you'd like. And bring my nieces.'

'I don't think I'd have enough coupons, Mary, to buy what they'd like,' I replied.

'Don't bother about coupons, I can soon fix that,' she said. 'Anyhow, where are you living now?'

'Still in Handsworth, Mary, you'll have to come and visit me some time. I'm sure the girls would love to meet you.'

'I'll try, but Kate, don't you think you should go and see Mum? I think she'd like to see you after all these years. How long is it since you saw each other?' she asked.

'It's been over ten years now. But I don't want to see her. I can't ever forgive her the way she treated me and my children all those years ago,' I replied bitterly.

'Don't be too hard on her, Kate. You'll find she's changed a lot lately, wouldn't you like to come with me some time and talk to her?'

'No, Mary, I won't. If you can forgive her, I can't. Ever since I was a child, as far back as I can remember, she was cruel and unkind. Maybe, Mary, she never led you the life she led me.'

'Don't be too sure about that, Kate. It wasn't all honey for me. I'd like to tell you about my life as far back as I can remember, when I was only a small child, and when you've heard it, Kate, you may understand why our parents were like they were.'

During that visit, and several visits I made to her over the next few weeks, Mary told me a lot about the family in the days before I was born: about a brief period of prosperity, when Dad had a good job and he was able to rent a nice house, and how they lost all that and had to return to the slums; and about the little brothers and sisters who had died, especially her beloved brother Sammy, who died of consumption. Through what she said I did come to have a better understanding of Mum and Dad, and why my family was as it was.

I still couldn't bring myself to go and see Mum, but when Mary told me how hard up she was I arranged to give Mary five shillings a week for her, on condition she didn't know where it came from.

Then, one afternoon while I was home, busy laying the table for my daughters' teas, I heard the front doorbell. When I opened the door, who should be standing on the step but my mother. I couldn't believe my eyes. She hadn't altered a bit.

'Well!' she exclaimed. 'Ain't yer gonna call me in then?'

'Yes, come in,' I replied.

As soon as she sat down I said, 'How did you find out where I lived?'

'Mary told me. An' thank yer fer the five bobs yer sent me,' she replied sharply.

'Would you like a cup of tea, Mum? I'm just getting it ready for the girls when they come in.'

'ow are me gran'children?' she asked.

'They're fine.'

'But why ain't yer bin ter see me? Yer can go an' see yer sister, but I suppose yer too stuck up now ter come ter see me.'

I didn't answer. I thought it was best not to reopen old sores.

'Will you stay and have a bit of tea?' I asked.

'No, not now. It's openin' time. But don't yow forget ter send me gran'children down ter see me, even if yow don't wanta come,' she added, slamming the door behind her.

When I told Mary about this visit she was glad some contact had been made. She also said she would talk to our mother and make arrangements for us to meet at her house. When the three of us met, later that week, I asked my mother if she would like to come and stay with me for a few days. She seemed all for it, and Mary too was pleased.

After that first visit Mum came to stay several times, but she always went back to her own house from Friday to Monday. I tried my best to make her feel wanted, but always towards the weekend I could see she was restless to be gone again. I realised she was eager to be back where she could be drinking with her neighbours. At the back of my mind I knew I'd made a mistake in asking her to stay. She was very bombastic towards me and my teenage daughters, and they didn't like her ordering them about. It was very hard to keep peace in the home while she was there. And she was a great worry during air raids. She would never go down the shelter when the sirens sounded, she just went upstairs with her bottles of beer and stayed in bed. ''itler ain't got me name on one fer me,' she'd say.

During the nights of April 1941 we had our worst bombing raids. The shelters were full to overflowing. But although many poor souls crouched in the corners afraid, many tried to keep up their morale by singing, to help drown the constant noise from the fighter planes above, the heavy gunfire and the falling bombs. We could hear the fire engines too, as their bells clanged, racing backwards and forwards along the streets, from dusk to dawn. When the bombing was not so heavy many of us voluntary workers would help the wardens to put out incendiaries, using buckets of sand, and dustbin lids.

There was one old dear who like my mother, didn't believe in going down the shelter. She always said she felt safer in her Anderson Shelter, which was only a piece of corrugated iron in the shape of a small igloo, covering a hole in the ground at the end of her garden. After the raids someone would always go and see if she was still safe. I remember very vividly one early dawn when I peeped down inside, to see her cat and little dog asleep beside her on the mattress. As I was going to give the message that she was safe, one of the wardens came running up. He told me that Camden Drive had been bombed, and that Mum and Mary had both been killed.

I tried to make my way to Camden Drive, past slimy, stinking mud, animal bodies and small fires from burning rubber, metal and rags, past buildings blown off their foundations, and men and women trying to salvage some of their treasured belongings. When at last I reached the top of the hill, neighbours from the district confirmed the bad news. But I still couldn't believe it, until I got half-way down the hill, and saw my brothers, Jack, Charlie and Frank, and my sister Liza, standing against the school wall weeping with many of Mother's neighbours. And there, lying on the floor with sacks covering them, were several bodies waiting for the ambulance to take them away. As I tried to look which ones were my mother and sister, the wardens quickly pushed me away and told me not any of them bodies were fit to be seen.

'Just remember how you last saw them alive, Kate,' my brother Jack said.

I was told that about twenty bodies had been dug up from cellars. One neighbour, who had a few cuts and bruises, said the bombing had taken them by surprise, before the sirens sounded. It was too late to go down the shelters, so people took refuge down their cellars. My brothers said there was nothing I could do now to help, but as soon as things were straightened out, they would get in touch with me.

The day of the funeral hundreds of people gathered from all areas beside the many coffins in Warstone Lane cemetery, where gravediggers were working day and night.

After the funeral I said goodbye to my brothers and my sister Liza, and walked home praying that my son John was still safe on the high seas. And that this was the last air raid we would witness. But there was a lot more to come, before that (never should have been) bloody war ended.

12

Fires, a Policeman and a Wartime Christmas

Each night, when the all clear sounded and we came up from the shelters, none of us knew what changes we would find to our homes. Many times I wondered, too, if my small workshop would be intact after the raids.

For most of the war my enamelling business was run by me and my daughters and ten young women. At one time my workers had to clock in before starting work. But when the war started in earnest I said they could forget it, I didn't mind how late they arrived for work, I quite understood their worries and sleepless nights. Some of the workers brought sandwiches to eat out at dinner times. But during the cold weather some of us would pool our rations. One would supply a few carrots, another a couple of onions, someone else some carrots or split peas, and whenever I could I brought a piece of meat. While the girls were working, and listening to 'Music While You Work' on the wireless, I'd prepare our dinner, put everything in the pot on the gas ring and let it stew away until it was time for us all to have a small basin full, with a piece of dry bread to mop it up.

That terrible morning after Camden Drive was bombed, I arrived at my workshop to see several firemen still putting out fires at the buildings across the street. I was scared to think what I would find as I climbed up those two steep flights of stairs, but when I entered the room, everything seemed to be in order. The girls were all busy doing their work, and listening to Tommy Handley on the wireless. Later that morning I prepared the meat and vegetables as usual, put them in the pot, and left them to simmer. Later, happening to go to the other end of the shop, I looked up and saw a gaping hole in the roof. At first I thought it must have been made by a piece of shrapnel. But then I looked around and saw another hole in a bench. When I peered down I saw an incendiary bomb resting on a ledge beneath the bench. I screamed out, 'Leave everything, girls! And hurry down into the street!' We were all down those stairs like a flash. But before I could stop her, one of the girls suddenly rushed back up the stairs again. She cried out, 'I'm goin' back fer me tin 'at an' gas mask.' A few seconds later she was back with them in her hand. But she was lucky, and so were we all, that the bomb turned out to be a dud. Often, later, we teased Lily about her attachment to her tin hat and her gas mask. But she never even smiled.

When the firemen said it was safe to go back upstairs, we returned to the workshop – to find it full of smoke. The dinner I'd left on the gas was burnt to a cinder, and so was the pot. But the kind woman at the tea shop nearby produced a makeshift dinner for us.

*

When we had an occasional rest from the bombing, usually all we wanted to do was catch up on our sleep. But one night during a lull, for a special treat, I took my daughters and two of their friends to see a show in town. It was late when the show was over, and we'd missed the last tram home, so we had to walk.

It was a lovely moonlit night, but the roads were icy. By the time we got as far as Hockley Brook we all wanted to pee. Looking around we couldn't see anywhere we could go. We were afraid to stoop down in the gutter, in case someone came along and saw us. But when we'd walked a little further, we noticed a low wall jutting out on the pavement. Dropping our knickers down over our ankles, we sat down on it. As we were giggling and peeing, from out of nowhere a policeman came towards us. We were all scared to move now, we could only sit there with our bare bums freezing and the steady stream trickling down the pavement for anyone to see. He said, 'You young ladies should be indoors at this time in the morning.' When I tried to explain we'd missed the last tram, he replied, 'Come along, then, I'll see you home.'

'Thank you, officer,' I answered quickly. 'I'm their mother, and we've only a few yards to go.'

I noticed he was smiling as he replied, 'Very well, mother, you'd better hurry along before you all freeze sitting there.'

As soon as we saw him stroll away, we quickly pulled up our wet knickers, but as we slid down from the wall we saw he was waiting and looking at us from the corner of the street. You couldn't see us for dust, as we fled up the Soho Hill. As soon as we got indoors we kicked off our wet knickers and made a mad dash towards the fire to thaw out our bums.

We laughed, later. But we suspected that policeman was probably laughing too!

*

One cold November day my brother Jack came to see me, and said if I'd lend him my old Austin Seven he'd give me some petrol coupons. When I asked him what he wanted the car for, he said he wanted to go to Henley-in-Arden market, where there were some live chickens for sale. I said he could take the car providing that I could come along too.

The old jalopy spluttered and rattled all the way, but eventually it got us there. Jack bought four hens and a cockerel, and I bought a turkey to fatten up for our Christmas dinner. I didn't know where I was going to keep the turkey. But when my brother suggested he'd take it home with him and bring it back on Christmas Eve, ready for the oven, I didn't trust him. I hadn't forgotten the pig he'd stolen when we went hop-picking when we were young, and I didn't think Jack had changed much meantime. So I refused.

I decided that the only place I could keep the turkey was in the coal-house outside. I moved what little coal I had, and set the turkey on some straw. My daughters named her Gertie, and grew very fond of her.

One bitterly cold night Jack borrowed the old car again and brought me back a sack of coke, which I mixed with the coal I had to make a roaring fire in the scullery grate. I almost forgot about Gertie until I went to feed her, when I suddenly noticed that the brick wall between the back of the fireplace and the coal-house was red-hot. Quickly I dragged poor Gertie into the kitchen, where she had to sleep that night, for otherwise she might have been cooked alive.

We were unable to risk lighting a fire in the scullery after that. A few nights later it was again freezing hard. So I put extra coal and coke on the living room fire and, as my daughters sat around warming themselves, I held a piece of newspaper up to the fire to help it along. Suddenly it was sucked alight by the draught and blown up the chimney. In no time at all, the chimney was on fire. Soot covered us like black snowflakes. We panicked and rushed outside. But the firemen arrived even before we had time to call the fire brigade; they had seen the flames and sparks shooting out of the chimney pot. The fire was so fierce, they had to go into the back bedroom and knock a hole in the breast of the chimney before they could put it out.

What a mess, and what a crowd of people we had outside looking in. And then, no sooner had the firemen done their job and left, when in walked a policeman. I recognised him at once. He was the same tall, handsome policeman who had seen us sitting on the wall, with our bums freezing. I felt so embarrassed. My only hope was that although I knew who *he* was, he might have forgotten who we were.

As he took out his note pad and pencil, he asked, 'When did you last have your chimney swept?'

'I never used this fireplace till tonight,' I replied.

While he was writing down all my answers to his questions, I saw him look up and smile at my daughters.

'And where's your husband?' he asked.

'I'm a widow,' I replied.

Suddenly he asked, 'Do I remember seeing you from somewhere?'

'No, I don't think so,' I answered quickly.

But he looked across at my daughters again, and he smiled more broadly as he said, 'Ah, I remember now. You were all sitting on the wall at the bottom of Soho Hill, late one night.'

I didn't answer yes or no, but tried to change the subject. 'Would you like a cup of tea, officer?' I asked.

'No, thank you,' he replied, 'but if you have a drop of something stronger I'd be very grateful.'

I hurried to the cupboard and brought out the remains of a bottle of Johnnie Walker that I kept for the wardens. I noticed that the girls had disappeared into the kitchen.

The policeman took off his helmet and sat down on the couch. He began to get very chatty, and asked how long I had lived there, how old my daughters were, and how long I had been a widow.

After he'd jotted it all down, he told me he had a wife and two young boys who were staying in Wales with his parents, until after the war.

'But you don't sound like a Welshman,' I said at once.

He didn't reply. He just stood up, and as he was putting his helmet back on my daughters came into the living room.

'Be good girls,' I heard him say to them, 'and don't let me see you out late at night again, doing what you shouldn't.'

They almost knocked one other over as they dashed back into the kitchen. And there they stayed until he had gone. I felt more embarrassed than ever now, and I was eager for him to go, before he asked any more questions. I was relieved when I saw him tear up his notes as he went down the path thinking all the time we'd been talking about how he knew what we had been doing that night as we sat on that wall, with our bare bums freezing as we giggled and piddled.

*

It was a few days before Christmas and snowflakes were falling fast when my brother came to see me again. As soon as he got indoors and took his wet overcoat off I said, 'Jack, I'm worried about Gertie.'

'Why, what's the matter with 'er?' he asked.

'I don't know, she hasn't eaten her food these last few days, and she sits in her corner all broody and looking so pitiful, as though she knows what's going to happen to her, and the children are upset too about having her killed.'

'Well, she's old, Kate, an' if I don't do it soon she'll die probably on yer later, then she'll be no good to eat, an' she'll 'ave ter be buried somewhere.'

'But you didn't tell me she was old!' I snapped.

'I didn't know till the other day. That must have been why she was so cheap,' he replied.

'Oh, well, you'd better start to do it now, before the children come home,' I said.

'I can't do it now, Kate,' he replied.

'Well, what have you come for?' I asked angrily.

'I was goin' ter ask yer ter lend me the car again.'

'Sorry, Jack,' I said, 'I've taken it to be overhauled and it won't be ready till after Christmas. If then.'

'Pity,' he replied sullenly. 'I could 'ave done yer a good turn.'

'What! Like the turkey you said was a good buy?' I said angrily.

'Sorry about that, Kate. Anyway, I'll come Christmas Eve morning and fix 'er fer yer,' he said, as he walked out of the house.

The next few days Kathleen, Jean and Mary (who was home for Christmas) tried their utmost to make Gertie eat. They even talked to her like you would to a child. But she just sat in her corner of the coal-house, looking broody and all forlorn, as though she knew what was going to happen to her.

It was still snowing when my brother came on Christmas Eve. While he sat in front of the fire smoking his pipe, the girls came in. As soon as they saw their uncle, Jean ran up to him and asked, 'Have you really come to kill Gertie, Uncle Jack?'

'Yes, luv,' he said. 'She's old and she'll die if I don't do it now. Anyway,' he added, 'it'll be a nice change fer you all ter sit down ter turkey instead of a couple of sausages.'

At once there was a crying match. But my brother explained to them why it had to be done, and I thought they understood. Still, I didn't want them to be anywhere near the house to witness the killing, so I gave them some money and sent them off to the pictures. While I worked in the kitchen, busily washing up and preparing the vegetables for the next day, Jack went into the coal-house and did what had to be done. Then I plucked the bird and began to clean it. When I put my hand inside it I pulled out one large egg in its shell, another almost ready, three yolks, and dozens of small eggs the size of peas. I put them into a basin to be made into custard, for pouring over the Christmas pudding. When I'd finished cleaning the turkey, I hid it in the larder where the girls wouldn't see it, until the next day when it would be cooked.

I was determined to make this a happy Christmas, for in those days no one knew whether we would ever see another one. On Christmas morning, while the girls were still asleep, I slipped up to the bakehouse in Soho Road with the turkey and paid a shilling for it to be cooked. When I got back I set the table with all my best china and glasses, and added Christmas crackers and four paper hats I'd bought at a garden fête. Also a few goodies I'd collected over the past weeks, and a bottle of port wine my brother Jack had given me for the loan of my car. I took up the girls' breakfast and their small presents, and I said they should stay upstairs until I called them down. When I had fetched the turkey from the bakehouse, I drained off the fat into a basin, put the bird on a dish, and put it in the oven to warm. Then, as soon as all the vegetables were ready, I called the girls.

I was pleased as they sat at the table drinking their port, laughing and smiling. But as soon as I put Gertie on the table and began to carve, there was another crying match. 'We don't want any!' they cried out, and sprang up from the table.

I did my utmost to persuade them to eat, but it was a waste of time even to try. I did manage to get them back to the table again to eat their Christmas pudding, which I could see they relished. But if they'd known the custard had been made with Gertie's eggs, they wouldn't have eaten that either.

After they went out to see their friends, I began to weep. What a waste of time and energy and money, I said to myself. I was too upset now to eat any of Gertie, either. So I wrapped it up and gave it to one of my neighbours who I knew had a lot of mouths to feed. When they asked why, and I tried to explain, the old grandad said, 'The ungrateful little buggers, kids are terday. They'll be glad to eat 'orse-flesh before they're much older.' (Little did we know, we already had.)

When I got back home I sat down again and wept, and after clearing the things away I thought to myself if only my brother Jack or Charlie had come that Christmas morning they might have persuaded the girls to eat some of it. But I felt alone now, and it was Christmas Day. Suddenly I couldn't think of anything else, only to put the crackers and the paper hats on the fire and take the rest of the port and a glass of whiskey up to bed. It was night-time when I awoke, with a fearful headache. I hurried downstairs and just as I was making myself a cup of tea, my daughters came in. When they said they were hungry, I snapped, 'You can be bloody hungry! You can have some bread an' drippin', but you can get it yerselves!'

Little did they know it was Gertie's dripping they were spreading on their bread, and I wasn't going to tell them in case there'd be another crying match.

Later in the spring Jack brought a dozen little chicks for the girls. They were so delighted they kept them in a basket while it was cold. But one morning when we came downstairs they all lay dead on the hearth. That was another crying match. After that I said, 'No more livestock in this house,' and if they wanted a chicken or a turkey it would have to be a dead one from the butcher's.

But I understood really how my daughters must have felt that Christmas Day. I'd have felt the same when I was a girl – though I wouldn't have dared refuse anything I was offered.

13

Sooty and Sandy

I managed to stick to the 'no livestock' rule for a while, but it wasn't easy. My daughter Jean was very possessive where animals were concerned, and often she'd bring home some stray cat or dog. Then I'd have to sort out who owned it.

One night my daughters were in bed and I was sitting reading the newspaper, when all at once I heard a sound like a baby crying. It sounded as if it was coming from one of the bedrooms, and as I opened Jean's bedroom door, I knew it was coming from there.

When I turned the bedclothes back, I saw a black kitten lying in Jean's arms, mewing for all it was worth. I felt angry to think she had disobeyed me. Just as I picked it up and put it on the floor, Jean woke up.

'What have I told you!' I cried out at once. 'No more livestock!'

'He followed me, Mum,' she protested as she sat up in bed.

'I've heard that before! Like the other cats and dogs you tell me follow you!'

'But it's the truth, Mum, I tried to shoo him away but he wouldn't go. I thought if I gave him a drop of milk he'd go away.'

I knew then we'd never be rid of it.

'Now, I want the truth,' I said. 'How long have you had it in bed with you?'

'Only a few nights, Mum. Please let me keep him,' she pleaded, as the kitten jumped up on the bed. As soon as I saw her tears flow, I began to weaken.

'I'll think about it. But you can't have it sleeping with you in bed, it's unhealthy. It can sleep in the kitchen tonight, then I'll decide what you can do with it in the morning. Now, lie down and go to sleep.'

I picked up the black kitten and took him downstairs, where I gave him a drink of milk. Then I put him outside to do his business. At the back of my mind I hoped he'd go back to where he came from, but after a while he began to meow louder than ever outside the kitchen door, so I let him in. I found a discarded old woollen jersey, and as soon as I picked him up and laid him down on it he snuggled up and went to sleep.

Next morning I told my daughter she had to try to find out who owned the kitten, but if no one came forward she could keep him. But I warned her it was her responsibility to teach him to be clean. The next day I bought him a basket to sleep in. And Jean gave him the name of Sooty.

As Sooty grew older, he began to stay out late. By then I was as silly as Jean, and I wouldn't go to bed until he was indoors. One night he didn't come home until one o'clock. I scolded him for keeping me up late. But he just purred and rubbed against me.

The following night he stayed out again. I waited for a while and called him, but no Sooty came. 'Very well,' I said aloud, 'you can stop out,' and I locked the door.

It was early in the morning when I heard him meowing outside the back door. I couldn't sleep now, knowing he'd be almost frozen out there, so I went down and let him in. But I was still angry with him for disturbing my sleep.

This went on for a couple of nights more. Then one night there was a caterwauling session of toms and she-cats under our windows, and the neighbours'.

I couldn't sleep, and nor could the neighbours. I heard windows being pushed open and all kinds of oddments being thrown at the cats, and I heard somebody say, 'Bleedin' cats, I'll drown the bleedin' lot on yer if yer don't get away from under my winda.'

After a while it went quieter, but I still couldn't sleep until I knew Sooty was back. As soon as I heard his cry I went down and opened the door. There he sat, looking so pitiful, and soaking wet.

'It's yer own fault,' I said as I dried him before I went back to bed.

I knew it was Sooty's nature to go out courting, but I had to do something about him staying out late. So I decided to leave my kitchen window a little way open for him to come and go as he pleased, so that I could get some sleep. This worked until one late night I heard a great din coming from the kitchen, and I went down to find Sooty and his girl-friend, a ginger she-cat from down the road, making love. I got the broom and swiped at them, and they both fled through the window.

'That's the last time I leave my window open, or let you in again when you stop out,' I said to myself. There was only one answer to the night prowling, I would have to have him castrated.

The following day I put him in his basket, and while my daughters were out I took him to the PDSA (the People's Dispensary for Sick Animals) in the Soho Hill. As I sat waiting my turn with other people with their pets, I began to weep. How could I do this to Sooty? I was just about to take him home again when the vet called me in.

When a little while later, the vet laid the unconscious Sooty in my arms, he said to keep him warm and watch for him to wake up, and then to give him a drink. I thanked him and when I asked him the fee, he said, 'It's voluntary, but if you'd like to put whatever you can spare in the box.' I dropped a half-crown in the 'Sick Animals' box and put Sooty gently in his basket and carried him home. When I laid him down on the rug in front of the fire I began to weep again. He lay there so still, I thought he was going to die. I thought, what was I going to say to my daughters. I couldn't tell them the truth, things like this were never discussed in front of children in those days. I sat and waited, hoping he would come round before the girls saw him. And a few minutes later, I was pleased to see him come to. Soon he was on his feet and walking, and he seemed to be his usual self as he looked up at me and drank his milk. But as the weeks went by, and I noticed he wasn't so frisky as he used to be, I began to be sorry again that I'd taken his little pleasures from him.

Then one day Jean walked in with a little all-black kitten in her arms. I was furious, and shouted, 'You're not bringing any more cats in here!'

'I'm not, Mum,' she protested. 'I've only brought him to show you.'

'Well! You can take it right back again to where you've had it from.'

'Mrs Wilks says her cat's got four, and three of them are just like our Sooty.'

'I don't care if they're like King Kong!' I replied angrily. 'Take it back at once. And if you're not satisfied with Sooty, I'll give him away.'

'I still love Sooty, Mum. But he isn't playful any more.'

'Well, he's growing older now, you can't expect him to play like he did when he was a kitten. Anyway, love, I can't put up with any more cats. I must have my rest. What with the air raids and getting up half the night, and one thing or another, I don't get much sleep. You can have anything else, but definitely no cats.'

Tears began to fall, but she didn't miss her chance. 'Can I have a dog, then, Mum?'

'I'll have to think about it. Now, do as yer told and take the kitten back.'

A few weeks after, I heard that Mrs Wilks had given the kittens away, but kept her ginger she. Later, after her house was bombed, she went to live with her sister in another district, but she didn't take her cat with her, she left it to roam the streets. Day and night that cat would whine outside our back door. I couldn't see her hungry, so I used to feed her out in the yard. Then one night it poured in torrents, and Jean began to plead for me to take her in. When I dried her with a piece of cloth, she nestled up to me. After that I couldn't let her go out in the rain again. So I gave her a home, and we called her Sandy.

Sandy too had to go to the vet's, for I made sure I wouldn't have any more kittens in the house. And from then on Sooty and

Sandy were content to sleep side by side, without any sign of lovemaking. They grew old together, and when they died I buried them beneath my kitchen window. Eventually Jean got her dog, but that was years later.

14

The Children Grow Up

My three teenage daughters were now growing up fast in mind and body. I knew I couldn't keep them under my wings all the time, but whenever possible I always took them out and about with me. I used to worry when they went out by themselves. There were lots of American troops in the district, and many young girls (and married women too) found them hard to resist, with their gifts of chocolates, cigarettes, silk stockings, and other scarce luxuries. Many a young girl was left holding his baby. I remember one of my neighbour's daughters had fallen this way. And I often think of how she said one day about her daughters, 'They make your arms ache when they're young, but they make your heart ache when they're older.'

One day I received a letter from my son, John, who was still serving in the Navy, to tell me that while he was on leave in Scotland he'd met a young Scots girl whom he wished to marry. I was very upset. I'd had other plans for John. I'd been hoping that as soon as the war ended he'd take over my business, so that I could care for the girls and the home. I wrote at once asking him to wait until the war was over, as they were both too young to think about marriage. But John wrote back to say that the banns had already been read. I went up to Scotland with my daughters, still intending to talk him out of marrying if I could, but when I got there I found I couldn't say anything disapproving. They looked so happy, and so much in love. After the wedding John had to go back to his ship. His wife stayed with her parents until he came out of the Navy when the war ended.

During 1944 my daughter Kathleen was married. I planned to give her a wonderful wedding, a better day than I had had. My one trouble was the food rationing. But again my brother Jack came to the rescue.

'If yer can lend me the old car again, I'll see what I can do,' he said.

So I lent him the old jalopy. He said he'd be back in an hour. I waited all that morning, getting more and more worried. All kinds of thoughts entered my head. Then about two o'clock in the afternoon he came in with another chap, both drunk, and laden with parcels of food.

Although I was pleased to see him, I was also angry. 'Where've you bin till now, our Jack?' I cried out. 'I've been worried stiff.'

As they dropped the parcels on the table, he managed to say 'It's all right, sis, but I got some bad news ter tell yer.'

'Well, sit down and tell me, before you fall down!' I replied angrily.

'When I drove back 'ere, the bottom of the old jalopy fell out and the grub fell inter the road. This chap 'ere,' he said, waving his hand towards him, "elped me ter pick it up and bring it 'ere.'

'Where's the car now?' I asked.

'We dragged it on some waste ground an' 'ad ter leave it.'

'Oh, well,' I replied, 'I knew it would happen one day. As long as you're all right, that's all that matters.' I thanked the young chap for his help and asked him if he'd like a cup of tea, but he said he was in a hurry to get back to work. When he called again, a few days later I invited him to the wedding, which was to be in two months' time.

My next worry was we couldn't hire a hall for the wedding reception: every possible room seemed to be booked for ARP (Air Raid Precautions) meetings. But a friend of mine who was a builder talked me into having the wall between the front room and the dining room knocked down and made into one large room. I later called it the lounge.

And in the end everyone seemed to have a jolly time at the

wedding. Piano-playing and singing went on far into the night, well after my daughter and her husband had left to start their honeymoon.

Later Kathleen and her husband, Jim, went to live in Scotland. After a while she wrote to say she wasn't very happy where she was living. I wrote back to say I was thinking of leaving the old house and buying another, and if she was still not settled they could come and take over the house in Waverhill Road. And when I bought my house in Landgate Road, and Jean and Mary and I moved there, Kathleen and Jim moved into Waverhill Road. A little later Kathleen came to work with me again. Then when Jim lost his job he came to work along with us. He didn't know the trade, but he was happy to do all kinds of jobs, and worked very hard.

It was of course a great pleasure to me that Kathleen and Jim had settled down so near. But many were the times I'd lie awake at nights thinking about my son John, on the high seas and perhaps in battle, and pray to the Good Lord above to keep him safe. There were now only my two younger daughters, Jean and Mary, at home with me. I dreaded the thought that some day soon they too would fall in love and leave me to be married. I knew I'd miss their love, excitement and laughter when I was left in this house alone.

I had had many offers of marriage over the years, but I hadn't been interested. All I had wanted was the love and affection and comfort of my children around me. But how foolish I was to think I could keep them by my side for ever.

My youngest daughter, Mary, was restless, always trying one job after another. One of her jobs was serving in a fruit and vegetable shop owned by a Mr and Mrs Hitchman in Hockley Street. Mrs Hitchman was kind to anyone really in need, but she was a very domineering woman, and very large, and I often felt sorry for her husband, Fred. He was so different, a weedy, hen-pecked little man.

Mrs Hitchman was sweet on my brother Jack, who was very plausible. And many times Jack would take her in her car to markets. She'd get all dolled up when she was going to see him. I used to hear customers whisper, 'Silly old cow! 'er's old enough ter be 'is mother.'

One day I told my brother how people were talking. But he said it was none of my business, or other people's. 'Let 'em talk,' he said. 'That's the only time I can get any black market off 'er, when I give 'er what she wants.'

I was furious at his attitude, and we quarrelled. I didn't see him again for a few weeks after that, but I knew really that, as he said, it was none of my business. So when I did see him again I thought it best not to mention it.

Then one day Jack's wife heard about their affair, and threatened to leave him. He never went near the shop again, nor was he ever seen taking Mrs Hitchman about. Whether he met her secretly I couldn't say. But he always had plenty of black market food.

During that period my daughter Mary came home one afternoon and said she'd seen a notice in Mrs Hitchman's shop window for a young girl to serve behind the counter. I knew if I refused to let her go she would go anyway, for she was very self-willed. So, to save any arguments, I let her have her fad out. I went to see Mrs Hitchman and we agreed on the wage, and that Mary would have her meals free. As food was still on rations, it was a help for me to save the coupons. But she had only been there about three weeks, when she came home one day crying.

When I asked her what was wrong, she said she wasn't having enough to eat, and that she'd been helping herself to bananas and couldn't find anywhere to hide the skins. When I asked why she hadn't told me before, she said, 'I was too scared, Mum.'

'Well, what *did* you do with the skins?' I asked.

'There's a big vase on the top shelf and when I thought she wasn't looking I threw them inside the vase. But it's getting full, and I was scared, and when she asked me to go up the ladder and reach down the vase, I panicked.'

'What happened then?' I asked, as the tears flowed.

'I ran up the stairs. As soon as I heard her talking to a customer I crept quietly down, but half-way down I met Mr Hitchman coming up and . . . er . . .'

'Go on, and what?'

'He pinned me against the wall. I knew what he was after. So I punched his face and pushed him down the stairs, and ran away.'

'But why didn't you tell me about this before? And why didn't you tell her you had the bananas because you were hungry?'

'I was afraid, Mum, because she'd know I'd stole them.'

'Oh. You knew you were stealing, then?' I snapped.

'Yes, Mum,' she whimpered.

'Very well, dry your eyes, and any time you get into any scrapes in future, come and tell me at once.'

'Yes, Mum,' she replied, as she dried her eyes.

Next day I called to give Fred Hitchman a piece of my mind. But he was nowhere to be found, and after that he always avoided me when he saw me. In the end I thought it would be better to leave things unsaid, to save any trouble which it would cause between him and his wife. After Mary left the fruit shop she went to train as a nurse at the TB Hospital in Selly Oak. She got along fine there, until she became tired of working all hours and left to try her hand at a hairdressing salon. Soon after Mary left the hospital the matron came to see me. She spoke very highly of Mary, and asked if I could persuade her to come back again. I said I'd do my best. But no matter how I tried for her to see reason, it was hopeless.

When she got dissatisfied with hairdressing, she tried being a conductress on the buses. Later she joined the forces, and she met and married her husband in Singapore. After the war, she and her husband made their home in Scotland. Later I had a letter from her to say they were going to live in America. Now Mary has four sons: two I have never seen. And I have only seen my daughter twice in twenty-seven years. For years I never heard from her, although I knew she recieved my letters. And I felt very hurt. But recently she has telephoned me a couple of times, which has been a great joy.

Over the years I have often asked myself if Mary still hasn't forgiven me for parting with her, when I left her at Dr Barnardo's.

15

My Second Marriage

My daughter Jean stayed at home longest, but I knew I would lose her too some day. And when she began courting I was often very lonely. I really felt I needed a companion and friend, someone to talk to of an evening. One night, as I was reading the *Evening Mail*, a knock came. When I answered I was surprised to see standing on the doorstep my brother Jack. I hadn't seen him for several months.

'Hello, stranger!' I said, sarcastically.

'Anythin' troublin' yer, Kate?' he asked.

'No, I just feel a bit under the weather,' I replied.

'Yer know what's wrong with yer, Kate, yer want to get out more and find yerself a man friend. 'ow old are yer now, forty?'

'Forty-two. Maybe I will, one day,' I said.

'Yer know sis, yer a good-looking chick and yer dress smart and –'

'Oh, go on, flatterer,' I interrupted, smiling up at him, as he stood with his back towards the fire.

He said, 'Well, there's many a decent chap who'd be proud ter be seen walkin' out with yer. So take my advice an' don't leave it too late.'

'I won't,' I replied. 'Anyhow, what's brought you here? I haven't seen you for months.'

'I've bought a second-hand car and I thought you might like to accompany me and the missus on a ride out in the country, termorra afternoon.'

'Thanks, Jack,' I replied, eager for the treat. 'I'll be ready when you call.'

It was a beautiful run, and I enjoyed the company – until we called in a pub to have a drink. The smoke room was crowded, it being market day. And when my brother kept showing me off in front of everyone, I felt embarrassed. I was glad when we left. As soon as we got outside to the car I lost my temper and stormed at him.

'If I want a fellow I don't need *you* to find one for me. I'll find my own! Thank you very much.'

'She's right, yer know, Jack,' said Rose.

He turned on his wife. 'Nobody asked yow ter poke yer bloody nose in!' he snapped.

I didn't want to be involved in an argument, so when I saw them get into the car I hurried down the lane. All the same I was glad when I heard the car coming towards me, for I had no idea where we were. There were no road signs to tell me which way to go – they had all been taken away in case of invasion. I got into the car. But I never spoke a word, until he dropped me outside my house. I was still angry. 'Next time you try pairing me up, Jack, don't! I can do my own pairing up, thank you!' I snapped. Then I went in and slammed the door. The car had just driven away, when Mrs Morgan, my next-door neighbour, called with a message. 'Come in while I put the kettle on,' I called out to her.

She was a kindly person and she had been very helpful when I first came to live next door.

I liked her, and I was glad of her company when I was alone. But she had one fault, she was an awful gossip, and knew everybody's business. When I had given her a cup of tea, I asked her what the message was.

'Oh, yes,' she said. 'I almost forgot. A young man called about an hour ago, an Air Force sergeant, said his name was Joe, and he knew you years ago. I asked him to come into my place and wait for you, but he said he had somewhere else to call, and he'd be back in an hour. Do you know who he is? He was a handsome fellow,' she added.

'I'm not certain who he could be, Mrs Morgan, but thank you for telling me.'

'Would you like me to wait with you till he comes?'

'No, thank you, dear,' I replied. 'I think I'd better see him alone. But thank you all the same for coming to tell me.'

'Well, don't forget to give me a knock on the wall if you need me,' she said as she went out.

As I tidied myself up, I wondered who this handsome fellow could be. I was soon to find out. A few moments later the bell rang, and when I opened the door there he stood.

'Hello, Kate,' he said, as he put his hand out for me to shake. But I didn't take it, I was too surprised he even knew my name.

'Sorry,' I said, 'I don't believe I know you. Anyhow, you'd better come inside.' (I was thinking of my nosy little neighbour, watching.)

He came inside and took off his Air Force cap, and I told him to sit down.

'Would you like a cup of tea? I've just made one. Then maybe you can enlighten me as to who you are,' I said.

He drank some of the tea, then he said, 'You sure you don't remember me?'

'I'm sorry, I don't,' I replied, still wondering.

'Well, we only met a couple of times. It was before you were married.'

Suddenly I remembered my first boy-friend, that I'd had such trouble with. He had been called Joe. Could this be him? But the stranger went on, 'You were about seventeen, and I asked your dad if I could take you to the Albion Picture Palace. And do you remember, you let me put my arm around you, but when I tried to kiss you, you slapped my face and ran out. I never saw you after that.'

Then I remembered. I began to smile, and he asked me what I was smiling about. I asked him, 'What became of the box of chocolates I threw at you when you tried to kiss me?'

'Oh, them? I gave them to the usherette.'

I knew then it had been a rotten thing to do, to throw his present at him.

We chatted for a bit, and I found that Joe had met my brother Jack, and that was how he knew where I was living. After a while he got up to leave. Suddenly I felt I didn't want him to go, in case

I never saw him again, so I asked him if he'd like to see my garden. He agreed, saying he'd got a few more minutes to spare. I took him through the back of the house and around the small pool we shared with other neighbours.

'Any fish in?' he asked at once.

'There's a few tiddlers, but mostly tadpoles. The trouble is, part of the year we get frogs on the front lawn, but they don't really bother me. They fascinate me when I see them hop from one place to another.'

As we walked back down the path and entered the kitchen, he took my hand. 'Kate,' he said, 'I hope you don't mind my asking, but could I call and take you out one evening?'

'I'd like that very much, Joe,' I said.

'What about next weekend?'

I'd been hoping he'd say the next day. But I tried not to be too eager to see him again. 'Yes, Joe, that will suit me nicely.'

He took my hand to shake, but then he said as he gripped it, 'Would you mind, Kate, if I kissed you – just once, before I go?'

I didn't answer, but as I put my face close to his he kissed me and squeezed my hand. That was the first thrill I'd had in years, and I hoped then that it wouldn't be the last, and that this would be the beginning of a long friendship.

I wasn't the teenager he'd known any longer, I was a grown-up woman with a family. But I needed a man's love and companionship. As he walked down the front path and waved to me, I felt sorry to see him go. He closed the gate and waved again, and I saw Mrs Morgan coming down her path. I knew she wanted to find out who he was, but I didn't feel inclined to gossip. 'Not now, Mrs Morgan,' I called out sharply as I went inside and closed the door. I needed to be alone and sit down to think things over. I wanted to see him again. But I couldn't help wondering if he was married. I should have asked him straight out, but I'd been afraid the answer would be yes. Anyway, even if it was, I thought, we could still be friends.

As I sat there thinking, I said to myself, if he was a married man, what if my daughters should find out? Whichever way it was, I would have to come to that decision later. I climbed the stairs and got into bed that night with a feeling that my life now was going to change for the better.

For several weeks after that Joe and I kept company, going to the pictures or to the theatre to see a show. But each time he kissed me goodnight before leaving me I wondered if he had a wife. I was still afraid to ask him, but I couldn't go on like this without knowing. So one night when he brought me home, I asked him to come in for a while and have a cup of coffee. He sat down and I handed him his cup, then I picked up courage to ask him – dreading the answer.

'Joe, I, er – wanted to ask you – er – are you – married?'

'I'm glad now you've asked me, dear. I should have told you that first day we met, but I didn't think it mattered then. But now it does, darling, because I've fallen in love with you.'

Now I knew the truth, I began to weep, and as he handed me his handkerchief I managed to say, 'I'm in love with you, too, but we mustn't see each other again after tonight, Joe.'

'Listen, Kate love, wipe your eyes, and try to listen to what I have to say. My wife and I have been at loggerheads ever since I came back from India. We're divorced now. Your brother Jack knows all about it. I'm only waiting for the divorce to be made absolute, and then I want to marry you.'

'Are you still living with her?' I asked.

'No. I'm living with my dad and my sister. *Will* you marry me, Kate?'

'I can't give you my answer now, Joe. Let me have a few days to think it over.'

'Very well,' he replied. 'But I hope you'll say yes, because I do love you, truly I do.'

'Joe,' I answered, 'give me a few days to think it over, then I'll give you my answer, one way or another. You'll have to go now before Jean comes home – and I can hear my nosy neighbour coming up the path.'

'Goodnight, then, Kate darling. But don't forget, I'll be coming for my answer. And whatever you may decide, I'll try and understand.'

I kept my tears back as he took me in his arms and kissed me several times. But as soon as I heard the door close behind him, I broke down and sobbed. A few seconds later the doorbell rang. I knew at once who it was.

'I can't see you now, Mrs Morgan,' I called out through the door. 'You'll have to call another time.'

As I heard her footsteps go back down the path I felt relieved. She was the last person I wanted to confide in.

I don't know how I got through the next few days, as I went about my daily routine. I was missing his fondness for me, and his company, and the things he used to say to make me laugh. I knew I was in love. But how could I tell my daughters that I was in love with a married man? Yet I knew I had to tell them sooner or later.

My brother Jack called to see me, and he asked why I was looking so worried. As soon as I tried to explain, I began to weep.

'Yer old enough to make up yer own mind, Kate, and now's yer chance to make something o' yer life. When Jean's married yer'll be left all alone. So think it over carefully. They're not children any more.'

'But, Jack, I'm worried about what the girls will say when I tell them I'm in love with a married man.'

''e won't be married when 'is divorce papers come through. Now, listen to me,' he replied sternly, 'yer never 'ad a 'appy life with yer 'usband befower 'e died. So now's yer chance. 'e's a good bloke, sis, so make up yer mind before it's too late. An' if yer want me to talk to the girls and explain, yer've only ter say.'

'Thanks, Jack. I think it would be best coming from me,' I said.

'Well, remember, Kate, yer've put them first in everythin' fer years, and now yer've the chance to be 'appy with someone who really loves yer. Make up yer mind before it's too late.'

After he left I began to think over what he had said, and I decided that as soon as Jean came home from work I would try and explain to her what I intended to do.

But when she came home I was still on tenterhooks how to begin. After she'd had her tea, we both sat by the fire. But before I could begin, she said, 'Mum, do you mind if Sam calls for me tonight? He wants to take me to the pictures.'

'But, Jean, I wanted to talk to you about something that I've been trying to tell you for some time.'

I was taken aback when she answered at once. 'Is it about you and Joe? Because if it is, I know what you're going to tell me.'

'Very well,' I replied. 'If you know, I'd better tell you what my intentions are. Joe has asked me to marry him.'

'Are you going to marry him, Mum?'

'Yes, as soon as his divorce papers come through.'

'I already knew he was married,' she replied.

'How do you know?'

'I met Uncle Jack the other day, and he told me everything. But if you do marry him, Mum, does that mean that he will live here?'

'Of course. I've already made up my mind, Jean.'

'But why, Mum?' she asked.

'I've thought all this over carefully. When you and Sam are married I shall be left on my own, and I couldn't face that again.'

'But we'll come to visit you, Mum.'

'That's not the same. When you are older and have a family you will understand what I mean. Now there's no more to be said. So you better get yourself ready if you're going to meet Sam.'

As she went upstairs to the bathroom, I began to feel sorry I had spoken so sharply. But soon the doorbell rang. It was Joe. I was just letting him in when Jean came down the stairs. When he began to wish her good evening, she didn't answer, but pushed past him and walked out. I felt very angry with her.

That same night I told Joe I would marry him.

But no matter how we both talked to Jean and tried to make her understand, we had many quarrels. A few days later she came home to tell me she was going to live with her sister. And as she was packing her belongings, I said. 'Very well, Jean, if that's what you want. But remember, if you wish to change your mind your home is always here – and remember,' I added, 'whatever happens, I shall always love you.'

A few weeks later, in February 1947, Joe and I were married at the registry office in Edmond Street.

16

Life With Joe

Joe and I had many happy years together. We had our disagreements (no one is perfect); but he was kind and considerate, and I loved him.

Some funny things happened as well. I remember one very bright moonlit night when we were first married and still living in Landgate Road. Something, perhaps the light, woke me, and I got out of bed to open the window wide to let in some air. As soon as I got back into bed I must have dozed off to sleep. But it wasn't long before I was woken again, by a kind of cooing sound. The light from the moon flooded the bedroom, so I didn't have to switch on the light. I was sitting up to see where the sound was coming from, when all at once I saw two large, bright eyes staring at me through the open window. Terrified, I slid down the bed beneath the bedclothes, and I pinched Joe's leg. 'Joe,' I managed to say, 'wake up! There's somebody staring through the window!'

Quickly he sprang out of bed, and as I held on to the tail of his shirt and followed him towards the window, we saw a large owl sitting on the window ledge, gazing at its own reflection in the glass. After Joe shooed him off and closed the window, we lay back in bed and laughed. My husband said that the owl, seeing its reflection in the glass, must have thought it'd found a mate.

But soon after that I got really scared. Ever since I'd come to the house, I'd been bothered by creaking noises in the bedroom at night. When I tried to explain to Joe he just laughed at me, saying I was imagining it.

'But, Joe,' I said to him one night, 'I can't sleep sometimes. It seems that there's someone in the room.'

'Yes,' he said, trying to put me off. 'It's us two.'

Then, one day while Joe was out, Mrs Morgan called to say the postman had left a parcel for me. I thanked her and, being glad of someone to be with me, I asked her in to have a chat and a cup of tea. As soon as we settled down together I began to tell her about the weird sounds I heard at night. But she just said, 'I'm surprised you've stayed here this long.'

'Why? What do you mean? I've only been here twelve months.'

'Well, didn't you know the house was haunted?'

'No, I didn't. But how do you mean, haunted?'

She asked me what bedroom we slept in, and when I told her the back bedroom, she said, 'Well, that's the room where a young woman murdered herself.'

'You mean she killed herself?'

'Yes, in that very room. And three families have lived there before you came.'

'And you told them what you've told me?'

'I didn't have to, they found out for themselves.'

Before she could tell me any more my husband came home, and when I told him what she had said, he forbade her to come near me or the house again.

Now I was more nervous than ever. I found it hard to sleep at night, and when I did drop off I awoke imagining all kinds of weird sounds. My husband said I was being foolish and superstitious, and we quarrelled. But I was now determined to look for another house. I walked for hours, until I saw one I liked that was for sale. I went at once to get the keys from the agent.

The house, which was in Uplands Road, was older than the one we were living in, but it was in good condition, and newly painted and decorated. It also had a long, well-kept back garden, where my husband could build a loft for his pigeons. Pigeon-racing was one of his favourite hobbies. After I had looked over the house, I asked the woman next door if she could tell me why the last people had left. She said they had been a very nice couple who had lived there for nearly thirty years, and had now gone to live in Canada with their son. I felt satisfied, so I went back to the agent, paid a deposit, and said I would call and make the necessary arrangements in a few days.

I hurried home, happy to think I would soon be leaving that house and those weird sounds behind me. But when I told my husband what I'd done, he flared up at me.

'The least you could have done was to tell me you intended to leave here. I like it here, and so would you if you hadn't listened to that bleedin' old busybody next door.'

One word brought up another. But I was adamant. We hardly spoke to each other for days, and when we did, we snapped at each other. I knew that I really should have discussed the situation with him, but I was desperate to move. The following week I made a start packing china and glass and other articles, which kept me busy during the day, but when night-time came, no matter how much my husband tried to convince me I was imagining things, I still couldn't sleep. Then something else happened. I had been awake for most of the night, as usual, but I dozed off just as dawn broke. Soon after, we both woke with a start, to find that the wardrobe door was wide open. Joe jumped out of bed and looked inside the wardrobe. He found that our savings had been stolen during the night. His wrist-watch had gone from the bedside table too. There didn't seem to be anything else missing. We pulled on some clothes and Joe went downstairs to phone the police, with me following very close behind him.

'I can't understand,' he said. 'I always make doubly sure that the doors and windows are locked before we go to bed.'

'I told you the house was haunted,' I cried out at once.

'Don't be foolish, Kate. Why would a ghost want a watch? And it couldn't spend money. It must have been somebody already in the house when I locked up.'

The police searched the house, but they found no clues to the intruder's identity. They left saying they would send someone to take fingerprints later.

As soon as it was daylight Joe went out into the back garden to feed his pigeons and, as I wasn't going to be left behind on my own, I went with him. But there another shock awaited us. Many of Joe's beloved birds lay dead on the lawn, and their eggs were strewn all over the path. Joe just went back into the house and wept. I too began to weep. Neither of us could understand why anybody would do such a cruel thing.

At least after this Joe too was pleased to get out of that house, and move to the villa in Uplands Road. But it took me a long time to get over my nervousness.

I'll never forget the first night we went to bed in our new home. We were both very tired after arranging some of the furniture, and we fell asleep as soon as we went to bed. But during the night I woke up with a fright. 'Joe!Joe!' I screamed out. 'There's a tall man standing beside the bed!' He sprang out of bed and switched on the light. I covered my head over with the bedclothes, scared to look.

'Where? There's nobody here,' he exclaimed.

When I managed to point to the bedroom door he became angry.

'What have I told you, about imagining things! What you saw was my dressing gown hanging on the back of the door. Now, let's get some sleep.'

After he got back into bed, we both began to laugh at my foolish fancy, and cuddled up together and slept.

A while later, one cold night in November, I switched on the electric blanket before getting into bed. During the night I woke up feeling very hot. Joe was restless too, and he'd thrown off the bedclothes. I tried to cover him up, but as soon as I pulled up the bedclothes a waft of smoke hit me.

'Joe!' I screamed out as I shook him, 'wake up, quick, the bed's on fire.'

He was out like a shot, so was I. I ran downstairs for a bucket of water, and when I came back he had already thrown the smouldering feather bed through the window into the yard below. That night we had to sleep on a mattress. Next morning, when I went into the bathroom to put my false teeth in, they weren't in the mug. I couldn't understand, for I knew I'd put them in water before getting into bed. Joe wasn't very pleased when I woke him up to tell him my teeth were missing.

'Sure you ain't swallowed 'em?' he snapped.

'Of course I ain't! I put 'em in the mug of water on the bathroom shelf.'

'Well, I didn't see 'em in the mug when I threw the water over the bed. Anyway,' he added, 'if they were in the mug you'll find 'em among the feathers! So now I'm going back to bed.'

In my nightie, and with bare feet, I dashed downstairs and out into the yard. I searched among the wet feathers for a long time, but in the end I found the teeth.

I went back upstairs and scrubbed off the feathers which were clinging to them.

Joe was still angry with me. 'No more bleedin' electric blankets I want to see in this bed. Or you sleep on yer own.'

I began to sneeze. I felt ready to weep.

'Now get yerself back in bed before you catch cold.'

When I got in beside him and sneezed again, he forgot his anger and took me into his arms. As soon as we got up we went to a furniture shop to buy another bed, but it was a week before they delivered it. Still, we were happy and contented sleeping in each other's arms on that hard mattress.

*

For most of our married life, Joe worked as a bookmaker's clerk. At first he used to take bets on street corners, but later he got a job taking bets in a Conservative club of which he was a member. Off-course cash betting was illegal then, but luckily for Joe he was never caught. Still, I was always on edge until he came home.

Working on commission, he did very well. On the days of big races, such as the Derby, or the Oaks, or the Grand National, he'd earn twice as much as if he'd been working in a factory (which he couldn't have stood, anyway – he never liked people giving him orders). Sometimes his commission at the end of the week would be over £100 (that was very good money in the forties and fifties). I didn't ask him for much, because I still had my small enamelling business. Be he never hesitated to buy me something he thought I wanted. He was always kind and generous. Unfortunately, though, he was a habitual gambler himself. I used to get very worried when he lost heavily on the horses or the dogs, but he always seemed to come out on top in the following weeks. When I tried to tell him that he should be more careful, his job wouldn't last for ever, he would reply, 'You won't go short. And as long as I've got me fags, and a few shillings in me pocket, and you, I'm happy.' But I didn't know what he had in his pocket. I knew he wouldn't tell me even if I asked.

One day he brought home a television set he'd bought so that he could watch the horses running on Derby day. By the time of the big race he was very excited. He'd already won over £30 on the first two races, and he'd put it all on a horse called Devon Loch to win the Derby. As soon as the horses started he got down on his knees and pulled the screen nearer to get a better view. Devon Loch was winning easily. 'Come on, you little beauty!' Joe kept yelling at the screen. When the horse was nearly at the post, its legs splayed out and it dropped dead. Joe went berserk. He picked up the television and slung it across the room.

I knew then it was time for me to vanish. I didn't come home till late that night, and by that time he'd cooled down. But he never stopped talking about that Derby horse. He always swore it had been doped.

Every Friday morning Joe would do his Littlewoods football pools coupon and post it on the way to his club, and on Saturday nights he'd light up his fags and watch the results on television. Once he won a fourth dividend, but he knew it wouldn't be much because there were such a lot of draws. The following Wednesday the letter came and when he opened it out fell a postal order for 2s.6d. He looked disappointed. As he went to sling it into the fire I took it from him and put it in the desk. A couple of weeks later he had got up early to light the fire and bring me up my usual cup of tea, when I heard him call up from the bottom of the stairs, 'Kate, what did you do with that postal order?'

'It's somewhere in the desk. Why?' I called down.

'Where's the key?' he asked.

'In my bag. I'll be down in a minute,' I replied.

As I opened the desk and gave it to him, I said, 'Surely you're not that hard up!'

'Of course I'm not. I thought of using it on the last coupon of the season.'

He didn't even study it, just filled in eight draws and went out and posted it.

As a matter of fact we both forgot all about it, and we didn't even watch the television that Saturday night. The following Wednesday we had a letter, and a cheque for £1,400. As soon as I saw it, I took hold of it.

'You're not having this to gamble with,' I cried out. 'If you do, I'm leaving you . . . And I mean it.'

He stared at me hard. But I was absolutely determined. I knew I'd given him something to think about.

'Very well, then, I'll put it in the bank,' he said.

But I still couldn't trust him. So I replied, 'It's not going into your bank. It's going into mine.'

It didn't stay there long. Soon after, Joe had a windfall on the horses, and won over £200. With that plus the pools money and the money we got for our house in Uplands Road, we were able to buy a new house in Rookery Row. And we had enough left over for a fishing holiday in Ireland.

17

Holidays in Ireland

Our holidays in Ireland were the happiest of all the happy times
we spent together. Joe was delighted by the plentiful coarse
fishing, and we both loved the kind, helpful people.

One afternoon as we'd settled down to fish beside the River
Shannon, two ragged little boys about the age of eight, with their
bare bums showing through their trousers and no boots or socks
on their feet, came running along the bank towards us.

'Ye want some worms, mister?' one cried out, as they came
near us.

'No, thank you, sonny, we've got plenty,' Joe replied.

'English? They're no good for our rivers. Ye want our Irish
worms if ye want to catch big fish, mister.'

'Yes, mister,' the other little lad piped up, 'we can go and fetch
ye some, mister, and ye'll catch bigger fish, mister.'

We felt sorry for them the way they were persisting, so Joe said
we could do with a few more worms, and off they ran. The two
little artful dodgers must have had the worms already hidden
behind the trees nearby. They hadn't gone but a few seconds
before they came back with a tobacco tin full of fat worms, which
we knew would be no different from our English worms.

Joe took the rusty tin and thanked them, and when he gave
them a few coppers they were delighted. But as soon as they ran
off we were pestered with several more ragged little urchins, all
trying to sell us their tins of worms for a penny each. I thought
then, those crafty little fellows must have made quite a nest egg
for themselves, if other fishermen bought their Irish worms. But

we didn't encourage them to pester us. We packed up our rods and moved to the other side of the river.

We sat down on a low bank where we had a long stretch of river to ourselves, and fished quietly for two or maybe three hours. Then, as my husband was turning around to put another worm on the end of his line, he saw another little ragamuffin.

'Here's another one of 'em!' he called out to me.

When I turned to look I felt sorry for the little mite. He looked a poor, neglected little chap. I would say he was about six years old. He was barefoot, and he had no shirt or jersey, only an old grey check waistcoat that was too big for him, and home-made trousers that looked as if they'd been cut down from a man's old ones. As he walked slowly towards us he kept hesitating, whether to come on or go back to wherever he'd come from.

Neither of us spoke, until eventually he made his mind up to come and stand beside me. After he had been watching for a few minutes he said, 'What are yer fishin' for, lady?'

'Well,' I replied, smiling at him, 'just a few fish.'

'Do yer mind if I sit down an' watch?'

'No,' I replied. 'As long as you keep quiet.'

He sat there watching the rods and lines in the water. After a while my husband came over and opened up the creel where we kept our sandwiches. As he took the lid off the tin he said, 'There's not much food left, Kate, but there's a piece of cake here if the little lad would like it.'

'Yes, please, mister,' he replied at once, as his big brown eyes opened wider, eagerly watching the cake being unwrapped. We took a few steps back up the bank in view of our rods, and when I handed him the piece of cake he thanked me and came and sat beside us again, as though he belonged to us. Whoever he belonged to, the little chap had nice manners.

As soon as he finished eating, and we had given him a drink of tea from our flask, we moved back and sat beside the rods again, and he sat down on the grass beside me. When I asked what his name was he replied cheerfully, 'Me name's Sean Murphy.'

'But you don't speak like the other little Irish lads.'

'No, me an' me mam come from England to stay with me granny.'

'What part of England?' I asked.

'Dudley, near the Black Country.'

'We're from England, too,' I said.

'We 'ave lots of men fish 'ere who come from England. But I've never seen a lady fisherman before.'

'Does your daddy fish?' I asked, smiling at him.

'No, me dad ain't with us, 'es back in Dudley lookin' after me three brothers and sister.'

'And how old are you?'

'I'm nearly seven,' he replied.

He was quite a little chatterbox now I'd got talking to him.

He told us his dad had been a prisoner of war in Germany and only had one leg, and that when he grew up he was going to be a soldier like his dad.

I said, 'You'll change your mind, son, when you grow up, for there's better things in life than being in the Army.'

''ave you bin a soldier?' he called out to my husband a few feet away.

'No, sonny Jim. I was a recruiting officer in the Air Force. Now, just sit still, I can see my line moving,' he cried out.

'If yer catch a big one can I 'ave it ter take 'ome ter me mam, mister?'

'Yes. Now, sit quiet while I try and land it.'

But whatever it was my husband was trying to wind in, it broke his line and got away. The three of us were disappointed, but he soon fixed the line again, and the little chap and I moved a few paces further away, so that we wouldn't disturb him, for I knew he liked to be quiet while he was fishing.

As I watched Joe light another fag, the little chap began to tell me more about himself and his mam and his granny.

'Me mam came 'ere to look after me granny,' he said. 'But now me granny's died an' we're goin' back 'ome after the funeral.'

'Oh, I'm sorry to hear about your granny.'

'I ain't, she used to beat me when me mam went out.'

'And why, Sean, would she beat you? Were you naughty?'

'Oh, no. She was very deaf an' sometimes when she 'ad 'er temper up she'd shout at me to get out of the way, an' if I wasn't quick enough she'd 'it me 'ard.'

'Did you tell yer mam?'

'No, I was too scared, an' she only 'it me after me mam 'ad gone out. One night I went inter the bedroom an' put lipstick and rouge on my face, like I'd seen me mam do it, an' as soon as me granny came up and saw me she gave me another beatin' and made me scrub it off an' sent me to bed without anythin' to eat.'

'But you should have told yer mam, Sean.'

'She made me promise not to, an' I did. Afterwards she put her arms around me an' cried, then she went downstairs an' brought me up a mug of cocoa an' a plate of cake, an sat on the side of me bed an' cried some more, an' said she was sorry, an' would never 'it me again. After that night she never did, a few mornin's later when me mam came 'ome, she found 'er in bed an' she was dead.'

I'd heard enough to put two and two together, so I changed the subject.

'Do you like this country, Sean?' I asked.

'Yes, I like the rivers an' the green fields an' all the animals, an' sometimes I go along with the farmers an' talk to their dogs an' the sheep an' the cows, an' when I grow up I shall come back an' live 'ere,' he gabbled.

'You do that, Sean, if that's what you'd like to do. It will be better than being a soldier.'

But who was I to tell him what he was to do? I might never see him again. He was not my son, though I was beginning to wish that he was.

While I was sitting thinking, suddenly he cried out, 'Yes, that's what I'll be, lady, a farmer!'

As I kissed his cheek, my husband called out excitedly, 'Bring the keep net, Kate. I've got a big one here, and I don't want to lose it this time.'

It was a large pike. As he landed it into the net he took the hook from its mouth, and threw it on to the bank.

'Is that for me, mister?' little Sean cried out as his eyes lit up.

'I think it's too big for you to carry home, sonny Jim.'

'But you promised, mister.'

When I saw the disappointed look on his face, I asked my husband how heavy he thought it was.

'Must be seven pounds, at least,' he replied.

But the little chap said, 'I've got some string in me pocket, an' if I can't carry it I'll drag it. Can I 'ave it now, mister?'

I asked him, 'How far away do you live?'

'At the top of the bank along the lane.'

'Well, if you'll go and bring some newspaper we'll wrap it up and carry it home for you.'

'Yer mean it lady? Yer won't throw it back in the river, lady?'

'No, we'll keep it for you. Now hurry up, and don't be long.'

I watched as he ran up the few steps along the side of the bank and out of sight.

'Enjoy yer little chat?' my husband asked as I sat down on the grass beside him.

'Yes, Joe, he's a lovable little chap. I feel as if I could adopt him . . . You know, Joe,' I added, 'I'd love to take him back home with us for a holiday.'

'Well, if you feel like that, love, perhaps you could ask his mum . . . . Where did he say he lived?'

'He said his dad and brothers and sister lived in Dudley.'

'Well,' he replied, 'that's not far from Handsworth, on the bus. But, again, I don't think it would be wise, love. What I hear the little chap say about his mother, I don't think we should get involved.'

'Maybe you're right, Joe. But I still feel sorry for him.'

Just then we looked up towards the steps and saw a middle-aged man holding Sean by the hand. The man was in his shirt sleeves, rolled up to the elbows, and as he came towards us I saw his round, very red face, and thick barrel chest and protruding stomach. Tied around his middle was a dirty apron. In his other hand he held a large paper bag.

'Good evening,' he greeted us at once. 'I bet that one give you a fight,' he added, as he looked down at the pike on the grass.

'It did that,' my husband replied.

As little Sean gazed admiringly at his fish, the man said, 'My name's Peter O'Connor, but everybody here calls me Pat.'

After my husband told him who we were, and shook hands, he told us that he kept the little pub a few yards away, at the top of the bank.

'But it's not seen from here. Little Sean says you're giving him the fish to take home to his mam,' he added.

The way he kept looking at the fish I had a feeling he wanted it for himself.

'Yes, we are,' I said sharply. 'We promised he could have it for his mum.'

'Now, now, don't get me wrong, missus,' he snapped back. 'I only came with the lad to carry it for him.'

Over his shoulder I saw Joe frown hard at me, a warning not to say another word.

Then Pat O'Connor turned to Joe and asked where we were staying. Joe mentioned the name of the place some distance away where we had taken a room, but added that we had stayed out too long and missed the train back, so we needed to find somewhere for the night.

'We haven't had time to look around for a place yet,' he added.

'I'm afraid you'll have a job to find a place around here, but if it's only for the one night me and the missus can put you up, bed and breakfast.'

'Thanks, Mr O'Connor, but . . .'

'Call me Pat, everybody else does.'

'Thanks again, Pat, but I really want to find somewhere we could stay for a couple of nights, I'd like to do some more fishing around here.'

'Well, I think we might be able to manage that. But we don't take anybody to stay as a rule.'

When I thanked him and tried to apologise for snapping him up, he said he understood, and asked my name. I said, 'Well, if I call you Pat, you can call me Kate.'

'Very well. If you'll both come along with me I'll try and fix you up with me missus.'

While we'd been busy talking, Sean had run towards the edge

of the river. 'Look, mister! Somethin's pullin' yer rods in the river.'

Quickly Joe grabbed hold of the rod and landed another large pike, almost as big as the first one. As he took the hook from the mouth of the pike, Pat O'Connor cried out, 'Don't throw it back, I'll take it back to me pub. The missus likes to stuff 'em.'

And so, after collecting our tackle we followed him and Sean up the bank on to the road above. Little Sean looked so proud walking beside the publican as he carried both fish.

'I'll have to leave you here, Joe, to stay with my fish, while I take this little chap home to his mam, he said, as he laid the fish on the piece of grass beside us. 'He only lives around the corner. I'll be back in a tick.'

The little chap thanked us again, and asked if we would still be there the next day. I said I couldn't promise – Joe liked to move about to explore different waters. But as I hugged and kissed him I felt my tears begin.

While we sat at the top of the bank waiting for Pat, we looked along the narrow, cobbled village street and saw several white-washed old houses, different shapes but all very small. To me, they all looked as if they were toppling sideways. I could hardly believe that people lived in them. On the corner stood the little whitewashed pub, with a sign over the door reading 'ALL ARE WELCOME INSIDE TO OUR HUMBLE DWELLING. P. AND M. O'CONNOR'.

There was not a soul to be seen, only a few stray cats who came sniffing at the fish. But I was scared by the odd look of everything, and was about to say, let's look for somewhere else, when Pat came towards us. Picking up the pike, he said, 'Come along, you must be starving, I know I am, let's go and see what the missus is cooking.'

We followed him across the cobbled path to the pub, where he took us through a large room which he called the tap room, then into another room which I supposed must be their kitchen. I stumbled a couple of times, swearing to myself as I caught my shin on the edge of an iron-legged table.

As soon as he lit the gas jets on the wall, I quickly glanced around. The place was old, but it looked clean and tidy.

'Sit yourselves down,' he said, as he pointed to a couple of horsehair chairs, 'while I slip upstairs and tell the missus.'

'Well, it ain't too bad, I've been in worse,' Joe said.

'Me too,' I said. 'If the bed's clean I don't mind.'

A few seconds later Pat entered with his wife.

'This is Maggie, my wife, and she says she can manage to put you both up for a couple of nights.'

'Thank you, Mrs O'Connor,' my Joe said at once as he took her hand. 'And this is my wife, Kate.'

'Pleased to meet you both,' she greeted us, smiling.

She was a large, buxom woman, with a round face, very big blue eyes and blonde hair which looked to me dyed, as it showed grey at the roots. She was very cheerful and asked if we would like a drink. Joe said, 'I don't drink myself, but I'd like a drink of lemonade, and Kate would like a stout.'

They bought in our drinks, with two glasses of whiskey for themselves, and sat by the table facing us. When Joe asked how much he owed, Pat said, 'That's all right, Joe, that's on us for the pike you give me and the lad.'

'Would you like to see the bedroom?' Maggie asked when we'd finished our drinks.

'Yes, please, Mrs O'Connor,' I replied.

'I'd like you to call me Maggie, everybody does, it sounds more friendly. If you'd like to go to the lav, it's on the landing next to your bedroom. And you'll find water and towel on the wash-stand.'

She lit the gas mantles on the landing and in the bedroom. The room was very small and almost bare, but clean.

'I'll leave you now to clean yourself up, then I'll have your supper ready.

When she'd gone I had a better look around.

There was an iron bed in the corner, and when I turned it down I was pleased to see it was clean and free from bed bugs. There was an old wicker basket chair beside the bed, a wardrobe which was very old and painted green, and a marble-topped washstand. Its legs too were painted green, and on it were a crock basin and jug (the jug filled with water), and a towel. There was no carpet of any description on the floor, just the uneven wooden boards with their knots protruding. Underneath the bed was a chamber pot. On the lime-washed brick walls there was nothing except a small oval mirror, and the gas bracket with the lighted gas mantle, which kept popping and hissing, throwing moving shadows across the room.

I stripped down and had a good wash. Unfortunately, I had nothing with me but my fishing clothes – a thick jersey and a pair of navy slacks – so I had to put them back on again. But after I spruced myself up and combed my hair I felt a bit more presentable.

When I went downstairs I found that the table in the kitchen was already laid out with cold mutton and vegetables, salad, hunks of bread and cheese, and a large jug of cider. While we ate, we chatted about who we were and where we came from, and got on quite friendly terms. When supper was over Joe went with Pat into the other room to have his fag, and I helped Maggie to wash up the supper crocks. After a while Joe came back to say he'd phoned through to the lodging house where we'd been staying, and he and Pat would be going early in the morning to pick up our cases. For that night Maggie kindly lent me a night shift which looked more like a bell tent, and Pat said Joe could use one of his nightshirts. And we went up to our bedroom.

I could have turned around three times without moving that shift. And I had to laugh when Joe slipped the shirt over his head – he looked like Marley's ghost. But soon I fell asleep. I woke in the night, to see Joe get out of bed, light the gas, and make his way across the room to the landing closet. Tripping along, lifting up his nightshirt with his hands, he looked so comical I couldn't stop laughing.

I was still smiling when he came back into the room. As soon as he lowered the gas, he snatched off the nightshirt and jumped into bed naked. When I began to giggle again, he snatched off my bell tent too. And that was the first time we ever made love together in the nude.

It was about seven o'clock the next morning when I woke again, to find Joe had already gone. It was a beautiful warm sunny morning. I washed and dressed quickly, picked up the night attire off the floor, and went downstairs. Finding myself in the front part of the pub, I looked around. This bit was more like a stores than a pub. There were groceries of every description. On the counter were weighing scales, cheese, tea, tobacco, soap, blacking, even bundles of firewood. You name it, they sold it. Walking a little further, I came to another small room with a bar, taps which drew the beer, and a small white crock barrel with a tap, and 'Irish Whiskey' on it in gilt lettering.

Then I found my way to the kitchen. Maggie soon came in from the yard, and she began at once to prepare breakfast on an open fire. She told me the men had left early, and would be back about ten o'clock.

While we were sitting having breakfast together, she began to describe what sort of people came into the shop.

'Does Sean's mum ever come in here?' I asked.

'No, not now. She's a bad 'un, that one, and when they bury her mother her and Sean'll be going back to Dudley.'

'Poor little chap,' I said, 'I felt very sad when he left us.'

'Yes, poor little feller. But he'll be better off when he goes back to his dad and the rest of the family.'

'I hope so, Maggie,' I said.

After breakfast I took a stroll along the village street. There were more people around this morning, and each and every one greeted me as I passed, some even coming out of their houses to say 'Top o' the mornin' to ye, mam'.

When I got back, Pat and Joe were waiting for me. Joe was ready and raring to go, with his rods already in his hand and his creel on his back.

'Can't miss the last few hours, Kate, get yer rods, I'm ready to be off,' he cried out.

'But what about some food, and a flask?'

'Maggie's put us up some bread and cheese, a piece of cake, and that bread and jam you liked.'

I got ready quickly, and we set off. Joe only had a few maggots left, but Pat said we would be able to get some bait from a friend of his, Paddy O'Leary, who had a boathouse at the other end of the village, so that was our first stop. The boathouse turned out to be just a corrugated covered shed. There was no one about, so we looked around. Over the wooden door was a sign which read, 'Paddy O'Leary, Carpenter. No jobs too large or too small'. Inside we saw new and old planks of wood and pieces of old furniture, and on a long, worn wooden bench there were nails, hammers, and a couple of hand-saws. Everything was cluttered up, and there was a thick layer of sawdust on the floor.

I was startled when a voice behind us said, 'Hello, there. Can I help ye?'

We turned to see a thick-set, elderly fellow, with sandy hair and a thick sandy beard. When Joe explained who we were, who had sent us, and what we were after, he said, 'I don't happen to have any maggots. I don't use 'em meself. But are you willing to have a piece of wasp cake? There's plenty of fat grubs, better than all your maggots. I won't fish with anything else.'

Joe thanked him and asked how much he was in his debt.

'That's quite all right,' he replied. 'But I'd be glad if you'd catch me a pike, or a nice fat chub.'

'I'll do that, and thanks again.'

Then as we went down the slope towards the river, he came after us. 'If you'll wait a few minutes, I'll get the old punt down and you can row where you want.'

He was so kind and helpful. The next thing we knew, he was wheeling the boat on an old rusty barrow towards the water's edge. We got in, Joe took up the oars and as we thanked Paddy again he gave the boat a push, and wished us good luck.

We found a peaceful, pretty spot in the middle of the river: green trees and wild flowers on the banks, not another soul about or any boats to disturb us, it suited us fine. When we had anchored, Joe said he would fix his rod up first while I got out the eats, and then he'd fix mine. I watched him take one of the grubs from the wasp cake, hook it on the end of his line, and drop the line in the water. Then we sat down, one at each end of the boat. But just as I handed him his sandwich, we heard a loud buzzing, and we looked up to see a swarm of wasps trying to attack us. I leapt up, dropping the flask and the sandwiches in the boat, and I

nearly tipped us both in the river as I sprang over towards Joe.
We must have looked as if we were trying to do some kind of a
war dance. As the wasps flew at Joe he twisted and turned, and so
did I. He took off his cap and as he swung a swipe at them the cap
left his hand and floated down the river. I yelled to tell him two
had settled on his bald patch, and he nearly tipped the boat over,
jumping in the air.

As we were swinging around and waving our arms in all
directions to swipe the wasps away, Joe suddenly turned and
shouted, 'What's in them bloody sandwiches?'

'Only what Maggie put up. The bread and cheese and the cake
and bread and jam,' I yelled back.

'Well, it must be that they're after. Throw it in the bloody
river.'

I did as I was told. But still they dived down at us. Just as I was
about to lift my hands to protect my face, I saw several swarm
down on the wasp cake that lay on the floor of the boat.

'Look, Joe, look, Joe!' I screamed, pointing. 'That's what
they've come after. Look!' I yelled again. 'There.'

Managing to get a piece of wet rag from his keep net, Joe
covered his hand and slung the grubs as far as he could into the
river.

'Well, we'd better make a move further up the river, before
they decide to come back,' he said.

As soon as we settled down again, Joe asked for the sandwiches.

'There ain't any. You told me to throw 'em in the river.'

'I meant the bread and jam, not the bloody lot!' he snapped.
'Well, I'll have a drink of tea.'

When I said I'd thrown the flask in too, he began to bawl at
me. I was almost in tears. When he said it was no use me blartin',
I swore at him and told him I'd never come fishing again. But
after he put his arm around me and said he was sorry he'd lost his
temper, I sat quietly in the end of the boat while he began to fish
again, using some of the few maggots he had left. But we had no
luck. He said we'd have to go back and get something to eat, and
after we might try the water where we'd fished the day before.

So we rowed back. As we tied the boat to the landing stage, Paddy came towards us. When Joe told him what had happened, he looked disappointed we hadn't brought him a fish.

'Didn't yer cover it over well out of sight?' he asked when Joe tried to explain.

'No, Paddy, I never give it a thought they'd swoop down on us like that.'

'No,' I piped up, 'and if I hadn't seen what they were after, we might have been swiping at them now, or I'd have jumped in the river.'

'Never mind,' Joe said. 'We'll know another time.'

'Not if I can help it,' I yelled at him.

I don't know what Paddy thought of me, but at the time I didn't care. I walked slowly away, leaving them talking.

As Joe and I walked back to the pub, he gave me a dressing down for loosening my tongue. I'd calmed down a bit by then, and, knowing that he had a worse temper than me, I thought better of making a sharp answer. We walked the rest of the way back to the pub in silence. But when we got back to our room he bent down and kissed me.

'Sorry I snapped at you, Kate,' he said.

'I'm sorry too. I didn't mean to be rude to Paddy after lending us his boat, either.'

'Oh, I think he understood. Anyway, let's hurry and get ready for something to eat.'

After we'd had our supper we went into the tap room, where we had a few games of crib with some of the locals. Then an old chap pulled out his tin whistle and played a tune, while another chap danced a jig. After which another sang 'Danny Boy'. Everyone in turn did something. When they asked me to sing, I was eager to burst forth. As I'd had a couple of glasses of whiskey and several of port, I was feeling very merry. I stood with my back to the counter and sang 'Kathleen Mavourneen', and then a song my brother had taught me when I was a child – 'Me little shirt me muvver made for me'. When I had finished, the men crowded around me asking for more. But I saw my husband frowning at me. 'No more, Kate, we've got to be up early in the morning to catch our train.' I was tempted to ignore him, but thought better of it. I didn't want to see him lose his temper among strangers. But I had the devil in me that night. I went over to everyone, and kissed them goodnight. Suddenly an old man put his arms around me and held me. He wouldn't let go, until my Joe came up to him and said, 'Now, now, grandad, watch yer blood pressure.'

When we got back to our bedroom I flopped down on the bed and began to giggle.

'I enjoyed myself tonight, Joe,' I managed to say.

'Yes, love, I could see you were, and I was watching that old man's hungry eyes on you!'

'Go on, yer jealous!' I giggled.

'Maybe I am. Now, get undressed and into bed.'

He helped me undress, and as soon as I crawled into bed I fell asleep. I didn't even feel him get in beside me.

The next day we had to get the train back to Dublin, where we were to catch the plane. We rose early and got packed ready to leave. Maggie was already cutting sandwiches in the kitchen when we went downstairs, while Pat was cooking our breakfast of ham and eggs over the open fire.

After breakfast Joe paid them, and we thanked them for their hospitality and promised to come again. I had just kissed them both, and we were turning to go, when we saw Paddy hurrying towards us with a parcel in his hand.

'I'm glad I didn't miss you, mam. I'd like to wish you luck on your journey home, and for you to accept this gift,' he said, as he handed me a cardboard shoe box. I began to smile, as I said, 'It doesn't happen to be another one of those wasp cakes?'

'No, it's something I've made for you to remind you of us all here in Arva.'

When I opened the shoe box I saw a wooden carving of the number of my house cut in an oval piece of dark oak. I threw my arms around him and thanked him, and as soon as I kissed him I felt the tears start, for they had all been so kind to us and I felt sad at leaving. But we had to go. They waved several times, and so did we, until we were out of sight.

*

Our next Irish holiday was the one we paid for out of what was left of Joe's pools win. I saw an advertisement in his angling paper, saying 'Come and stay at the Lakeside Hotel for plenty of good fishing.' It sounded just what we wanted. And we persuaded my eldest daughter, Kathleen, who had recently been widowed, to come with us.

The holiday didn't start too well. When we arrived in Dublin we found we had missed our train, so we had to find somewhere to stay for the night. Everywhere was dark, the streets were badly lit, and we didn't know where to begin looking for a place. But finally a local directed us to the Railway Hotel. When we got there we found it was a dilapidated old pub. It wasn't much to our taste, but we couldn't roam the streets till daybreak, so we decided to take pot luck. As we entered we saw it had no carpet on the floor, only wet sawdust. There was not a soul in sight, but we could see there must have been plenty of people there earlier, for the tables were strewn with empty and half-filled glasses of beer. The room which was supposed to be the bar smelt of stale beer and tobacco smoke.

As soon as Joe called out 'Anyone there?' a thick-set, middle-aged man popped up from behind the counter. With his flat broken nose and one cauliflower ear, he looked like an old prizefighter. His shirt was wide open at the front and showed a thick chest and protruding belly covered with sandy-coloured hair, and below his stomach hung a wet, greasy apron.

When Joe asked him if he had any rooms, he said that the place was almost full with a wedding party, but he could fix us up with a couple of rooms. Joe thanked him, and paid him, and a young lad appeared out of nowhere to show us upstairs.

We followed the lad up two gas-lit flights of stairs, almost tripping on the worn lino. He showed us a double room for ourselves and a small single room opposite, which was to be Kath's. The rooms were bare and shabby, but seemed clean

enough. In our room there was an extra single bed, as well as
our double one. We were tired from travelling all day, so we
went straight to bed, and to sleep. However, I hadn't been
asleep long when I heard the wedding guests had returned. They
were running up and down the stairs, yelling and laughing. I
was mad, and felt like jumping out of bed to tell them to be
quiet. But I shook Joe instead. 'Wake up, wake up!' I kept
repeating.

'Now what's the matter?' he cried out, yawning as he sat up
in bed.

'This ain't a hotel! It's a bloody madhouse,' I yelled at him.
'Why don't you get up and put yer trousers on and tell them to
have a bit more respect for people?'

'They probably don't know we're here. Anyway, let 'em enjoy
themselves, they ain't bothering me.'

'But they are me. And I'm going to tell 'em so!'

As I went to get out of bed he managed to pull me back.
'You're mad. We don't know these people, they might be rough
if you interfere with them. They'll soon get tired, and now let's
lie down and get some sleep.'

We lay down again. Joe was soon snoring. I covered my head
with the bedclothes, hoping I could drown his noise and theirs.

After a while the noises died down. I uncovered my head and
looked at my wrist-watch. It was almost midnight. Soon I dozed
off.

I hadn't been asleep long when I woke with a start, to hear
loud rumbling noises in the distance. At first I thought it was
thunder, but as it came nearer and louder, the whole room
shook.

I screamed out, 'Joe, wake up! Joe, wake up!'

'What's the matter now?' he cried out angrily.

'I'm scared. There was such a loud rumbling noise, and the
room shook.'

'Oh, go to sleep. You must be dreaming,' he said, as he began
to yawn.

'Listen, there it goes again . . . you'd better put yer trousers
on and go across the landing and see if Kath's all right.'

But he'd only just got his trousers on when the door was flung open, and in fell Kath in her nightdress. She slipped on a loose floorboard and it flew in the air, a chair going up with it.

'Whatever's happened?' I called out.

'Mum, there was such a terrible noise, sounded like a building falling down! Or thunder. But the second time I heard it, it was a train, come right past my window! I was so scared, I thought it was coming into the room. And I'm not going back there to sleep.'

Joe jumped back into bed, and covered his head over.

'Well, Kath, you'd better manage in that bed across in the corner, and mind you don't tread on that loose board again.'

I tucked her in and got back into bed myself, but we neither of us slept. Joe was snoring loudly. He must have had plenty of bruises the way I kept digging his ribs, but he'd still turn over and continue snoring.

We were all glad to see the dawn. We got up before five, and hurried to get dressed and away. I left Joe swearing as he was trying to shave in cold water, while I went across the landing to help my daughter pack her belongings.

In the daylight, that room looked so small. I hadn't noticed before that the head of the bed was against the window, which I saw had been nailed down. All I could see when I looked out was a brick wall a few feet away, and railway lines almost level with the window.

When we'd packed everything up we took all our luggage and went down to the dining room for our breakfast. Sitting near the counter there were four tough looking Irishmen, who kept eyeing us. When one of them came towards us, the proprietor stepped in front of him and said who we were. The fellow replied, 'Oh, I thought they were gate-crashers.'

We ignored them. But they still stared. Then the waiter brought in the breakfast. On each plate was a rasher of fat bacon, two fried eggs and some mushrooms, all floating in grease.

'Come on,' my husband whispered, 'let's go, we can't eat this.'

We picked up our luggage and got up from the table. The bar tender asked if there was anything wrong; any other time my

husband would have kicked up a rumpus, but he just made the
excuse we had to hurry or we'd miss our train.

As we walked towards the door I looked back and noticed the
four men dash across to our breakfast and begin to devour it.
They were welcome to it.

We had to eat somewhere though, the three of us were
starving. We hadn't eaten since three o'clock the previous
afternoon. Soon we came to a small tea room in a side street, and
we were lucky, the man was just unbolting the door. As soon as
we entered we ordered a large pot of tea and a dozen cakes. When
he saw us eating hungrily, he asked if we had been travelling all
night.

'No,' replied Joe, 'but I believe we would have been better if we
had, instead of in the place we've just come from.'

'And where might that be, if I may ask?' he enquired kindly.

When Joe told him, he just stood and stared. 'You must mean
Big Mike's. My God!' he exclaimed. 'But I didn't think anybody
was put up there now. I heard someone tried to kill themselves by
going through the bedoom window on to a railway track.'

'That accounts for the windows being nailed down, then,' I
said. 'And we hardly slept a wink for the racket. And the
breakfast they brought us, we had to walk out and leave, it was
just swimming in grease!' I added.

'You poor buggers! Just wait a few moments, I can hear my wife
in the kitchen. I'll see if we can rustle up a breakfast.'

We never enjoyed a breakfast more.

When, later that day, dirty, weary and very tired, we arrived at
the Lakeside Hotel, we found we had come from the ridiculous to
the sublime. We had never expected it to be such a grand hotel.

Looking down at myself, in my travelling slacks and jersey, I
said, 'We can't go in there, Joe, looking like this.'

'And why not?' he snapped. 'You answered their advert, and I
sent the deposit. So come on!'

I fully expected we would be refused entrance, but we had only
just stepped inside the lobby when an elderly gentleman dressed
in plus fours came and wished us good afternoon. As soon as Joe
said who we were, he replied, 'Oh, yes, you've come for the

fishing. Just leave your luggage, I'll send the porter along to show you your rooms.'

I couldn't believe our luck. The hotel was fit for royalty. Joe and I had a beautiful room overlooking the garden, and Kath's room overlooked the lake.

We bathed and changed, and did our best to look presentable for dinner, but we hadn't brought anything at all suitable for a hotel like this. So next morning Kath and I left Joe to his fishing while we caught the bus to Limerick to do some shopping.

We visited several shops, and bought a mac, sandals and three dresses each. Then we bought some fruit to have for our picnics. On the way back we were pleased to find that the bus was only half full, so there were a couple of spare seats for our heavy parcels. And we sat back to enjoy the journey. But at a stop only about half-way, we were surprised to see all the passengers leave the bus. We still sat there, but then the driver called out to us. 'All off!' We looked at him dumbfounded.

'I said, all off!' he repeated.

'But we've paid our fare to go all the way,' I replied.

'Well, we only go this far. We have to go back and pick up the five o'clock passengers. So you'll have to wait here until we come back.' he replied irritably.

As we collected our parcels I snapped at him, 'Well, if this ain't Irish, tell me what is.'

'Irish, Scotch, Welsh or bloody English,' he snapped back, 'you'll have to wait here till I return.'

And there we stood in that lonely lane, with not a soul to be seen. There was only one little shop, which was closed. And next door to it a small whitewashed cottage. We were plaiting our legs for a toilet, but there was no sign of one, so I knocked o൧ the door of the cottage to ask. A grey-haired old lady answered, and when I asked if there was a public toilet near she replied, 'You won't find any in these parts, my dears, but you're welcome to come inside and use mine.'

When we entered, Kath and I couldn't believe how small the living room was. She led us into an equally small space she called the kitchen, and pointed to a corner. 'In there, but mind you don't bump yourself.'

There was only room behind the door for one of us and once you sat down on the lavatory seat you couldn't close the door. As the little outhouse faced the street, anyone passing would have had a full view.

After we had been, we thanked her and went to pick up our parcels and the bag of fruit. But she said, 'Would you like a cup of tea, dears? I've got the kettle on the fire.'

We were very grateful and thanked her. While we waited for the tea I asked how often the buses ran.

'Buses?' she exclaimed. 'We only have one bus in these parts, and that only runs high days and holidays. It should be returning to pick you up in a few minutes,' she said as she looked up at the clock on the mantleshelf.

When we had finished our tea, my daughter asked how much we owed for it.

'You're very welcome,' she replied. 'It's not often anyone calls. But,' she added, 'I would like one of your oranges.'

As we picked up our parcels, my daughter gave her two oranges and a couple of apples for her kindness. Just then we heard the bus chugging up the hill. The old lady kissed us both, and as we went towards the bus, she waved and called out, 'God bless you both, my dears.'

We waved back and climbed on to the old bone-shaker. This time there wasn't a seat to be had, people were packed like sardines, and we had to stand with our parcels all the rest of the journey.

As soon as we got to our hotel and up to our room, Joe greeted us with, 'Where the bloody hell have you two been till now? I've been waiting over an hour. And you'd better get yerselves cleaned up before the dinner gong goes,' he added as he walked out of the room.

'I'd better go and change, Mum, he's in one of his moods,' my daughter said as she left the room.

'Very well,' I replied. 'I'll get ready too, and let's put on our new dresses we've bought.'

I was ready before Kath, and as Joe was already so upset about our being late, I thought I'd better hurry down rather than waiting for her.

When I arrived in the dining room, he was sitting at the table, waiting.

'Well,' he asked more pleasantly, as I sat down, 'why were you late?'

I began to smile as I said, 'You won't believe this when I tell you, Joe. It's really funny now I come to think of it.'

'Try me,' he said.

When I told him our tale, he too couldn't help smiling.

'Well, I suppose you have to expect anything to happen in these villages. They still keep up their old traditions.'

'Did you manage to do a spot of fishing, Joe?' I asked.

'No,' he replied. 'I walked about half a mile along the river and got my rods ready to fish. But then I saw a couple of chaps fishing for salmon. I felt a bloody ninny. We should have explained when we wrote what kind of fishing we did. Anyhow,' he added, 'we'll have to move on and find another river.'

I tried not to look disappointed. I would have enjoyed a bit more of the comfort and kind hospitality this hotel provided, which I'd never been used to, not to mention the luxurious food and surroundings.

'But, Joe,' I said, 'Kath and I like it here. Let's stay a couple more days, please.'

I saw the look of disappointment on his face, so I didn't say any more until we had our coffee. He said then, 'Well, if you two want to stay for a couple more days, I'll see the manager and explain we'll be leaving at the end of the week.'

The next day we went playing crazy golf and putting, with some of the guests. But I could see Joe wasn't enjoying the games and I felt very selfish, for I knew what a fanatic he was about his fishing. However, after a while he happened to get in conversation with one of the guests who had been a prisoner of war, and he obviously found that more interesting. While they were talking, Kath and I took a stroll along the country lanes.

It was a beautiful warm sunny day, and we must have been

walking for about an hour when we saw an old tramp coming towards us. His battered old trilby stood at an angle on his head, his grimy toes peeped out of his old boots, and his ragged coat and trousers were tied together with a piece of rope. His matted hair hung to his shoulders, and his face too was covered with hair. You could just about manage to see his eyes. But that was not all we saw. As he came nearer, we saw that his flies were wide open, and the end of the rope which held his trousers together was also twisted around his 'John Thomas'. We couldn't believe our eyes. We both began to titter, and my daughter managed to say, 'Is that what they call a shillelagh?'

'I don't know, but whatever it's called, he'd have a job carrying that thing under his arm.'

As he passed he must have known what we were tittering about. He turned around and winked. We never ran so fast in all our lives.

When I told my husband that night, he said he wouldn't let us wander alone again.

Next day the three of us were walking down another lane when we noticed a couple of cards lying in the path. We picked them up and saw they were racing cards.

'There must be some kind of horse-racing here,' Joe said. 'Come on, we'll go and enquire.'

Further along the lane we met a farmer, and when Joe asked him where the racing was he replied, pointing across a field, 'Over that stile yonder and across the meadow. You'll see it.'

So over the stile we went, and when we got into the field we saw it was a donkey derby.

I've never seen anything more comical than that donkey derby. There were eight donkeys of all sorts and sizes, some that could do with a good feed, others with pot bellies. Their jockeys were young lads who looked no more than twelve years of age. Each lad wore a well-worn white cow gown, three sizes too large, which almost dragged the floor, and on his back was a card with his name. Gordon Richards, Lester Piggott, Fred Winter, Harry Wragg, and other famous names, were in that donkey derby. After a hustle and bustle, the lads managed to get their donkeys into some sort of line. The rules were that no jockey was allowed to mount his donkey until the starter dropped his flag. Once the flag had been dropped there was absolute chaos as the lads tried to mount. Then they were off – or some of them were.

Two donkeys refused to budge, and were disqualified. Three more were already half-way down the field battling it out, when one decided he'd had enough: up went his hind legs, and off fell his rider. There were now only two donkeys left in the race. The one that was leading, seeing some blackberries in a hedge, decided he'd stop and have a feed. And when his jockey dug his heels in him and tried to pull him away, he kicked up his hind legs and the jockey went head first over the hedge. That left one pot-bellied donkey to plod along to the end of the field and back. Some people cheered, others catcalled, and Joe lost his half-crown. But it was well worth it for the fun.

Next day we heard there was some dog-racing nearby, so we decided to go to see that. The dog track was just a small field. There were ten dogs racing and each one was a mongrel, what we called the 'Heinz varieties'. There were long-haired, rough-haired, short-haired, wire-haired, and some with no hair at all. Each owner stood in front of a piece of canvas holding his dog firmly by the collar. Suddenly one owner called out, 'Black Beauty, where are you!' I looked down and saw the little black mongrel brush against my leg as he ran towards his owner.

'Kath!' I cried out, 'that's an omen, I'm going to back him.'

'Don't waste yer money,' I heard Joe snap. 'Anything can win. It's just a matter of luck.'

But I ignored him, and Kath and I hurried to put our couple of bob on Black Beauty to win. The man who was shouting the odds smiled at us. 'You're sure that's the one you want, missus?' he said.

We nodded. He gave us our tickets, and we went back to join Joe in the crowd and wait for the race to start. A piece of rabbit skin tied to the end of a piece of wire went around the field once, just to get the dogs keyed up. The second time it came around the owners let go of their dogs. Suddenly the dogs began to fight. Several flew up in the air, and there were balls of fur flung everywhere. A couple more just looked on. But there was little Black Beauty, running after the rabbit skin. He looked back once, as much as to say, 'You can all carry on, I'm all right.' He won the race and my daughter and I were the only two who walked up to that bookmaker to pick up our winnings, of five shillings each.

The next day was Saturday. We packed our luggage, said goodbye to everyone and started our travels again. We had decided to head for Athlone, where the coarse fishing was said to be good. Kath and I were sorry to leave the Lakeside Hotel, but Joe was pleased at the prospect of doing some fishing.

When we arrived in Athlone there was a bad thunderstorm, so we took shelter in a shop doorway. The owner of the shop, whose name was Mr Foye, invited us inside. When Joe asked him if he knew where there was a picture-house where we could go for a couple of hours, until the storm passed over, he replied, 'There's only the one next to the police office around the corner. I go meself sometimes. It's not much of a one, but it'll shelter you from the storm.'

'Would you be so kind as to let us leave our bags here until we come back?' Joe asked.

'I'm sorry,' he replied, 'I'm about to lock up. But if you like you can leave them next door, where I have my office. The old lady who lives upstairs never closes the front door, so you'll be able to pick them up when it suits you.

We thanked him for his kindness, and after putting the luggage next door we hurried from the rain around the corner, where we saw a large double-fronted house which seemed to have been converted into a cinema. Its windows had been bricked up and painted green, and in the glass fanlight above the door was written in black letters: 'Local Picture-House Prices four pence five pence and nine pence'. There were no posters outside to say what was showing. We took a chance and walked in. Sitting on a chair in the dim-lit hall was an old man who took our money: we paid nine pence, for the best seats.

The film was already showing when he directed us to our seats, which were hard and uncomfortable. I thought, if these were the best seats, what were the cheap ones like? I noticed too that the place was almost empty. To our disappointment, the first film was the Keystone Kops. However, we watched it through, hoping that the feature film would be a bit more up to date. But the next film was another silent, Charlie Chaplin's *The Kid*, which I had seen nearly forty years before. Joe fidgeted about, lighting one cigarette after another, until eventually he fell asleep. Half-way through the film he began to snore. I kept giving him digs, hoping to shut him up. After a while he opened his eyes and grunted, and then everyone in the house must have heard him, as he said loudly , 'Come on, I've had a bloody 'nough of this rubbish, let's go out and see if it's stopped raining.'

As we felt our way along the darkened gangway and out into the street we were glad to see the rain had stopped. But when we got to Mr Foye's office to pick up our luggage, we found the door locked. Joe went mad. He swore, he shouted, he banged and kicked the door, until a police inspector from the station next to the picture-house came to see what the noise was all about. When we explained who we were and why we were there, he said he couldn't understand why the old lady had locked the front door. 'It's always left open in case Mr Foye comes back late. Anyway,' he added, 'if you like to wait in my office I'll see if I can find him.'

We followed him inside, where there sat a very large, red-faced constable.

'Make these people a cup of tea, Tom. I'll be back in a minute.'

It took Tom a few seconds before he could ease himself out of the chair. 'Old achin' bones,' he said, as he shuffled to put the kettle on an old rusty pipe stove. We were just drinking our tea when the inspector came in with Mr Foye. He was all apologies when he saw us, and offered to drive us to our lodgings. But when we explained that we hadn't had time to look for a place, he drove us to some people he knew who put us up for the night.

Next morning after breakfast he brought our luggage and, apologising again, he offered us the use of his boat, if we wanted to fish the lake. We thanked him. In the end, Joe went out on the lake, with Mr Foye's son and another young lad to row him.

There wasn't room in the boat for five, so Kath and I stayed on shore. We thought we would clean up Mr Foye's boathouse while we were waiting, to show our appreciation of his kindness. The boathouse was really an old disused railway carriage that had been converted. All around the walls hung fishing rods, nets, and all kinds of fishing tackle. In the centre stood an old wooden table and two small wicker chairs, and against the wall was a marble-topped table where there stood a spirit stove, a tin kettle and an enamel teapot and some odd cups. Everywhere was thick with dust and grime. We got some water from the lake, and set about giving the place a clean, as best we could. We even went out and picked some wild flowers and put them in a cup of water in the centre of the table. Then we went for a walk. When we came back half an hour later we were surprised to see my husband and the two lads waiting for us. When I asked why they had returned so soon, Joe said he hadn't got enough bait to last any longer. He thanked the boys and gave them a couple of shillings each, and we went back to the digs to collect our belongings.

All the way Joe was sulking and swearing, saying all the time, 'I wish I'd gone back to Arva! At least the fishing was good. Yes, we should've gone back to Arva. My bleedin' holiday has been bleedin' spoilt. Waste of bleedin' money. Best we pack up and go home!'

I knew it was not for me to answer. On our way to Dublin to catch the plane back to England, he cooled down.

As soon as we arrived home and sat down, I said, 'Joe, next year, I think it would be better if you went to Ireland by yourself, and I'll take my holiday somewhere by the sea.'

'If that's what yer want, Kate. See what next year says, and we can make up our minds then.'

The following week I went with him to his fishing club, where we met his friend Jimmy Budd and Jimmy's wife, Elsie. Jimmy was a fishing fanatic, just like Joe.

'Enjoy yer fishin', Joe?' Jimmy asked as soon as he saw him.

Joe hadn't much to say about our last holiday, but when he started talking about the wonderful fish he'd caught in Arva, Jimmy was all ears. Soon we had made a plan that for our next

Holidays in Ireland 147

holiday we would all go to Arva together, Jimmy and Elsie, and Joe, Kath and me. This pleased me. I knew Joe would enjoy his fishing more with someone like himself for company. I wrote to Pat and Maggie to ask if they could put five of us up for a week, and I had a reply to say that now they had two extra rooms, and we'd be welcome to come any time.

*

When we arrived in Arva we went straight away to the shop-fronted pub. Pat and Maggie met us on the doorstep, and as soon as we had introduced Kath and Jimmy and Elsie they took us into the tap room for a drink. It was too late to begin fishing, so the two men said they'd make an early start in the morning, and when we'd had supper we spent the rest of the evening playing dominoes with the old boys.

Next morning the men set off very early. Kath, Elsie and I decided we'd go back down the lanes and explore. As I remembered there was not much for us to see or do, but luckily we came across another donkey derby, and we were well entertained, watching and laughing at the capers the donkeys and the lads performed. It was a beautiful hot summer's day, and we stayed out till the early evening. When we got back to the pub we found that Joe and Jimmy were back before us. As we sat having our supper, Pat said, 'There's a fishing contest going out tomorrow morning if you're interested. It's only five bob, and the money prizes are good.'

'Where do they start from?' Joe asked eagerly.

'From the hall at the bottom of the village. But,' he added, 'it's only for fishermen, no women are allowed.'

'That's all right,' I said a once. 'The donkey derby's still on, we can go there till you come back, can't we?' Kath and Elsie agreed.

Early next morning we were all ready to see the men start from the village hall. I've never seen such an excited and happy assortment of fishermen. They all scrambled up on the farmers' hay-carts, hauling up their baskets, rods and wellies, and struggling to get the best sitting positions. Joe and Jimmy were up there with the rest, waiting for the shire horses to start. Then all at once from around the corner came an Irish bagpipe band, in their full regalia. And to the music of the bagpipes the hilarious procession started off. Everybody came out of the little cottages to wave and cheer.

Once they were out of sight we went along to watch the second day of the donkey derby, but we found it had been cancelled. So we decided to walk along the river instead. A little way along the bank I found I needed a pee. There wasn't a soul about, so while Kath and Elsie walked on in front I took down my knickers. But I'd only just begun to pee when I saw some cows coming down the lane. I'd always been afraid of cows (indeed of almost all four-legged animals except dogs and cats), and I took fright. Dragging my knickers (now wet) after me, I climbed over the hedge – and landed on my back. I looked up to see several goats coming towards me. I screamed for all I was worth. Luckily for me, the goats turned around and fled. Kath and Elsie, hearing my screams, came to the rescue and helped me back over the hedge. I laid my wet knickers on the grass and, while I was sitting there waiting for them to dry, my daughter asked me why I'd been screaming. When I told her she said, 'If you'd have waited you'd have seen the cows go over the footbridge.'

'But what about them goats in that field?' I asked.

'The way you screamed was enough to frighten a herd of elephants!'

No sympathy from that one, I thought.

That day we decided to go back to the pub and have our dinner. In the afternoon we went for another walk, and by the time we got back we could hear the bagpipes in the distance. The fishermen were returning with their bags of fish to weigh in. There was a lot of commotion and grumbling, as each one weighed his catch. My husband said he'd won the third prize, which was £2. But it was decided that locals had won first, second, third and fourth. Joe and Jimmy knew it was a fiddle, but as Joe said, 'Who were we to argue with a crowd of the locals.' They'd had a good day's sport. And Pat was pleased with the two pikes, four large bream and a chub that they brought back. Joe and Jimmy often brought fish to Pat, but we never saw any of it again. Whether he sold them or cooked them or stuffed them, we never knew.

The men went out very early the next morning. When we came down later we were puzzled to see that the shutters were still closed.

'Is it a storm we're having, Maggie?' I asked

'No,' she replied. 'My shutters are still up because it's market day.'

We thought no more about it until we went outside.

'Close the door after you, Kate!' I heard her call out after us. 'I won't be opening until this evening.'

Outside it was broad daylight and the sun was shining, with the promise of another warm day. As I looked up and down the narrow street. I saw that every little shop and cottage had its windows boarded up. Then I looked along the lane, and saw that coming my way were cows, bulls, horses, goats and sheep, all being led to the market.

I stood there petrified. My daughter and Elsie just laughed at me and walked away. Quickly I turned back and rang the bell, hoping Maggie would open the door and let me inside, but there was no answer. In terror, I crouched down between two low walls, afraid even to scream in case I drew the animals' attention. When they had passed by I came from behind the walls and rang the bell again, but there was still no answer. So, checking that the coast was clear, I made an effort to go and join the others by the river.

Every animal had freely left his load behind on the cobbles, and some had splashed up on the boarded windows. The stench was terrible. I had to pull up my skirts and hold my nose, as I goose-stepped to find a dry cobble to plant my feet on.

When I got to the river and explained, they just laughed. But I didn't see anything to laugh at, at the time.

Later, as we came back to our dinner, we saw people sloshing buckets of water over their boards, and others with water and brooms swilling down their front doors and the gutters.

In spite of the cattle problem, I was very sorry, and so was everyone else, when the day came to pack our luggage and get ready to leave, and catch our plane back to Brum. We wished Pat and Maggie goodbye, and we promised we would come again the next year. But Joe and I never saw Arva, or the friends we had made there again.

As we were walking towards the end of the next village, we saw four men lounging against the wall of another small pub, similar to the one we had just left. The priest was walking along the street too, and when they saw him coming towards them, they almost stood to attention as they raised their caps and said 'Good mornin', Father.' He just nodded in reply. As soon as he had passed on, a hand suddenly came from behind the door and beckoned them to come inside. How quickly they dashed in, almost knocking each other over.

18

A Working Retirement

In 1963 I was sixty, and I decided to sell my business and retire, so that I could stay at home and have more time with my husband. I put the money in the bank, and for a while we lived comfortably on the commissions Joe earned. But a few months later his employer sent for him to say that now off-course betting had been legalised she was going to open up a betting office where the punters could go and put on their bets and hear the results, so she wouldn't be needing his services in the club any more. She offered him a job working behind the counter, but he said he wouldn't work inside for no gaffer. Although I did my best to persuade him, he was adamant.

'I'll find something,' was all he said, when I asked him what he was going to do.

But when he came home late one night and said he'd got a job at Perry Bar Stadium, cleaning and feeding the dogs and taking them out for exercise, we began to quarrel.

'Can't you find a better job than that?' I snapped.

'Well, I ain't working in a factory, if that's what you mean!' he replied angrily.

Then one night he persuaded me to go and see the racing. I saw enough that night to know I didn't want to see any more. One young chap had put all his money on a certainty (so he was told). It came in last. I saw him kneel on the ground and punch it several times, shouting out 'It was doped! The bloody dog was doped!' People crowded around him, asking if he'd had a fit. I never went to the dog track again.

Each night Joe came home late we quarrelled. He'd got in with a gambling crowd and lost more than he earned. Foolishly I helped him out and paid some of his debts, but he just went on gambling. Until at last I made up my mind to do something about it.

During my retirement, several of my old customers had come to see me and asked if I would help out by doing some enamelling at home. It seemed to me that if I could persuade Joe to work with me it might keep him away from the gambling crowd. I put it to him.

'It's up to you, Kate, if that's what you want,' he said.

'It's not only up to me,' I replied angrily, 'I'm asking you! Would you help? And if we don't agree, we'll have to think of something else. But I'm telling you one thing now, Joe, you're to give up gambling or I'm selling up and leaving you.'

'Very well,' he said. 'I'll try.'

We built a workshop in the garden and had the gas and electric put in, and then we started to work together on the enamelling. Joe gave up going out gambling. I didn't mind him having a small bet once a week on the phone – I realised how miserable he would be if he couldn't have one little squander – but I knew and he knew how far he could go. We worked together happily each morning. In the afternoon, we went to Summerfield Park, where he taught me how to bowl. During the months that followed I won many trophies in prize money and we joined Handsworth Victoria bowling club, where later I was made Captain of the Women's Team. Later still I became Captain of the Warwick-shire Ladies' Team.

These were happy years. Until I began to worry about Joe's cough. I knew he was almost chain-smoking, but each time I asked him to cut down, he became very irritable and bad-tempered. One day he complained about a pain in his chest and while he lay in bed I rang for the doctor. When he came he had Joe taken into hospital straight away. He'd had a heart attack.

I visited him in St Chad's Hospital the following day. But the next day while I was getting ready to visit him, he walked into the house, saying 'If I'm going to die I'll die at home.'

I was too shocked and upset even to answer him. After that he smoked more than ever. And one morning he collapsed on the floor. The doctor and the ambulance came at once, and Joe was taken to Dudley Road Hospital. When he began to improve, he phoned me each night, telling me he was now getting better and that I was to bring him some fags. I refused. But someone must have taken him some when they visited, and when the sister found out she warned him of the danger.

Late one night Joe phoned me, sounding very upset. When I asked him what was worrying him, he said 'Kate, you'd better bring my clothes.'

'Whatever for?' I asked.

'Never mind what for. Bring me my clothes. I want to get out of here!' he snapped. Then he added, 'What chance have I got when yer doctor drops dead in the ward?'

I rang the sister at once, but could get no reply. Next morning, after a sleepless night, I went to the hospital to visit him, and when he had calmed down he told me what had happened. Apparently the doctor had indeed had a heart attack and died while he was doing a ward round. Other patients too said the ward was all topsy-turvy when they took their doctor out on a stretcher.

Towards the end of the week Joe was discharged. He had been given some heart tablets to take, and I was pleased to see he was making an improvement. But he still smoked heavily. I knew it was useless now to try and persuade him to give up. A few weeks later I had to captain the bowling team in Manchester. When I asked him if he was coming with us, he replied, 'Not today, Kate, some of the chaps at the club have asked me to make up the team to bowl away. But I'll have yer tea ready by the time you come back home, love, and don't forget,' he added, 'I want to hear all about yer bowling.'

Then we kissed each other and waved goodbye. Those words were the last he ever said to me. That same evening when I arrived home from Manchester I was told that my husband had died while playing on the bowling green at Dudley.

*

It has now been over fifteen years. But I still miss him. More so than ever now. And I wish he were still here today.

Many times during the bowling season I watch the couples playing and think to myself how lucky they are that they still have each other, that they are able to talk to each other and share their worries and troubles. During many cold winter evenings I sit alone and think of those days and nights when we would pull up our armchairs close to the coal fire and make toast on the end of the fork. Sometimes later we would sit and play cards or dominoes, or do a crossword together until it was time for bed. Or he would pick up a detective story and read to me.

It all seems so sad, when you lose someone you love.

But I hope and pray, when the Good Lord opens up His book, and calls out my name, maybe I shall meet all my loved ones again.

Who knows?